All
Is
Self

JOSEPH P. KAUFFMAN

May all beings everywhere,
whether near or far,
whether known to me or unknown,
be happy.
May they be well.
May they be peaceful.
May they be free.

JOSEPH P. KAUFFMAN

CONTENTS

INTRODUCTION

Taking an honest look at the state of the world today, we can see that there is plenty of chaos, destruction and disharmony. Humans harm or kill one another because of their skin color, religious beliefs, or sexual orientation. We neglect, cheat, and compete with others to get ahead. We cut down the forests that provide our oxygen, pollute the rivers that provide our drinking water, contaminate the air that we breathe, and are destroying the very planet that sustains us.

We have a deeply rooted belief that life is a constant struggle, that nature is a force to be conquered, and that every non-human element is meant to serve and benefit human beings. Thus, we mine the planet for its resources,

1

in order that we may sell them and make a profit. We kill billions of living beings every year because of our belief that they exist only to provide sustenance for us. We have no care or regard for the natural world, because really, we see it as our enemy—as something to be fought with, as something to be used, and as something to be overcome and exploited.

What has produced such a destructive and disharmonious way of thinking? What has brought about this worldview in which we see life as a constant struggle? In which we fight against nature, fight against each other, and fight against ourselves? What has allowed us to completely neglect the well-being of others and the planet, focusing only on our personal well-being? What enables us to feel justified in harming others, or feeling as though we are more important than others?

All of the problems we face today as a society are the result of human activity. We are the cause of the destruction that we are doing to ourselves and to the planet. Our actions are preceded by our thoughts, and so the root cause of all the chaos in the world comes from our thoughts and beliefs about the world and about who we are. It is from our way of understanding the world that we relate to the world, which in turn determines how we behave in the world. With this understanding, we can see that the chaos in the world is but a reflection of the chaos within our own minds.

The idea that we operate against nature has its origins in our belief that the self, the thing we call "I", exists as a separate entity, an isolated and independent being that lives apart from nature. We regard it as self-evident that we exist as separate, self-contained beings, living out our individual dramas, while everything else—particles and cells, bacteria and minerals, plants and animals, humans, the planets, even the food we eat and the air we breathe, exist as something distinct and entirely separate.

What appears to be a vast and complex worldwide situation of external conflict, has its roots in a simple and subtle internal cause. We do not really know who we are. We have confused our true nature with an illusory identity created by our minds. Humanity as a whole is suffering from a case of mistaken identity, in which our idea of who we are is limited to our belief in being separate and isolated entities.

We have identified ourselves with our bodies, our names, our culture, our race, our gender, our sexual orientation, our careers, our social image, and so on—all of the things that divide us and encourage this belief in separation—and in doing so, we have overlooked the reality of who we are.

Every culture has a story, a narrative, a myth or a worldview under which they operate. This cultural narrative describes who we are, what life is, and what our purpose is. The Quileute natives of La Push, Washington, for example, believed that their tribe descended from the changer—a shapeshifting entity—and this dominant worldview shaped their every thought and action. The Incans of Peru believed that the deity Wiracocha rose from Lake Titicaca, and made mankind by breathing into stones. The Greeks believed that the world arose from Chaos, their name for the void of nothingness, from which arose Gaia (Earth) and all of the other Gods of the Universe.

Each culture has a dominant narrative or worldview that shapes the way they think and act. To the people of these cultures, their narrative is seen as fact, or is so widely accepted that they don't even notice its existence, as to them, it is simply the way that things are. A cultural narrative acts as a lens through which we see the world, and from this way of seeing the world, comes our way of acting in the world.

So, what is our cultural narrative? What are the beliefs that shape our understanding of ourselves and the world we live in? What is the story that we live by? And is it possible for us to see this story as a story? Or is it so deeply engrained in our way of thinking that it is simply impossible to look at objectively?

There are two prevailing narratives of our culture— the most widely accepted tells a story of us as separate and isolated beings, living in a random and insentient universe made of matter, which is interacting chaotically, and from this random and lifeless universe of inert matter, through an accidental and improbable process of evolution, life emerged. The second prevailing narrative still tells a story of us being made of matter, only in this narrative we did not come to being through a process of natural selection and evolution, but instead we were created by an all-powerful deity.

These two narratives shape the ways in which our society functions, because they shape the ways in which us as individuals perceive the world, and thus how we act in the world. As with any narrative, it is something that most of us aren't really aware of, it simply colors our perception without our recognition.

As powerful as these cultural narratives are, they are purely mental, based on belief, and only have power when we give them power with our energy and attention. We have the capability of taking a step back and observing these narratives, and seeing them for what they are. In doing so, we can become free of the stories that shape our worldview, and can then open ourselves up to seeing the world in an entirely new way.

When we change the basic belief structures on which our worldviews are standing, we can change the very world that we live in. Right now, our cultural narratives suggest we live in a world in which our individual lives are of little significance. They promote a worldview in which our survival is dependent upon competition and a struggle to gain resources at any cost. Our cultural narratives have created a world in which we fight against each other, and fight against the natural world of which we are intricately bound in order to survive, and so, we have created a world in which we are rapidly destroying ourselves in a deluded attempt to save ourselves.

If we are ever to be free of the confusion and destruction that is our current way of life, we need to stop and take a moment to observe the beliefs that shape our understanding of ourselves, and ask with honesty, sincerity, and genuine curiosity whether these beliefs are serving us, and whether or not they are actually true.

When someone has a habit that harms their health and makes them sick, all that medicine can do is temporarily mask the symptoms or prolong the process of illness, but until that person stops doing what is causing them to be sick, they will never be healed. Likewise, while it is important to focus on the external issues we face as a society, such as the corruption in politics, destruction of the environment, the inequality of the rich and poor, etc., none of these problems will be solved until we address the root cause of the problem.

The greatest thing we can do as a culture, is not to revolt against the many injustices we see in the world, but to inquire into our cultural beliefs, to question the narrative that we live by, and to ask ourselves sincerely if this narrative is true, for this is really the cause of the many injustices in the world, and until we understand the problem at its root, we cannot really do anything but mask the symptoms or prolong the process—like putting a bandage on a wound instead of treating it.

My purpose in writing this book is to draw attention to the fact that it is our culturally inherited beliefs and our definition of who we are that causes us to suffer, and that if we can question these beliefs, and discover the truth of who we are, we will have freedom and peace. For we are not separate, isolated beings, like our culture leads us to believe. We are all strands in the web of life, parts of the greater whole of nature, and more than that, we are the whole of nature expressed as individual parts.

If we can realize this fundamental truth—that our true self is the whole of nature, and that all beings are a part of our self—we can have peace and harmony on Earth. From this new understanding of who we are, we will act accordingly. When our actions reflect our understanding of oneness, and have in mind the benefit of the whole, then every action will be one that benefits all beings. But to accomplish this, we have to be able to look at our cultural narratives, question the stories that we live by, and change this worldview of separation by realizing that ultimately all is one. All is self.

1   PERCEPTION

"When you change the way you look at things, the things you look at change."

—Max Planck, Founder of Quantum Theory

Have you ever felt sad or depressed, and in that state, it seemed like the whole world was sad and depressing? Or have you ever been full of joy, and everything around you likewise seemed beautiful and joyful? Was it reality itself that was depressing or joyful? Or was it just your thoughts, emotions, and beliefs *about* reality that made it appear depressing or joyful in that moment?

We fail to realize just how much our internal environment shapes our experience of our external reality.

Everything we perceive "out there" is influenced, shaped, and colored by what is happening "in here." If I believe myself to be separate and isolated from everyone and everything, then the world appears to be a frightening and dangerous place. But if I see myself as connected to everyone, then I will feel at home in the world, and will feel like I belong to nature. Then the world is seen as a very beautiful and peaceful place.

The world appears differently according to our individual perception, which is shaped by our own beliefs and past experiences. Take a beautiful woman, for example. Such a woman is seen variously by different beings. To her father, she is a daughter. To her children, she is a mother. To her husband, she is a wife. To a tiger, she is not so much a beautiful woman but is instead a tasty meal. If this woman is perceived uniquely according to one's individual perception, could we ever know her true nature? Or are we always limited to our personal perception, shaped by our individual beliefs and experiences?

We can use anything as an example in this way. Some people find a certain food to be delicious, while others find that same food disgusting. Some enjoy certain types of music, while others are repulsed by it. Some may enjoy one activity, while others find that activity unamusing. Everything that we experience is limited to our individual perceptions.

Reality itself is free from the qualities that we impose upon it, and it is hard to say if we could ever experience a reality free from our personal conditioning, as it shapes the very lens with which we view reality. It is also impossible to say for certain if there even is a reality that exists apart from us and our perception of it, as we could not experience it—so how could we know?

Whatever the true nature of reality is, it is clear that our experience of reality is vividly shaped and influenced by the beliefs that we have about reality, the beliefs we have about the world, and the beliefs we have about ourselves. But what is it that we believe? What is it that determines our current worldview? And how did we get these beliefs?

Most of us never question our perception of reality or the beliefs that we have. Instead, we tend to think that our view of reality is the way reality actually is, and we live our lives accordingly. We have accepted the beliefs and opinions of others—of our culture, our media, our family, our teachers, religions, scientists, etc. We ask them about the world and we are satisfied with the answers they give us, taking them as being the absolute truth.

But I think it is important for us to inquire into our own experience of reality, to come upon realizations for ourselves, and not to just take the beliefs of another's to be our own, regardless of who that person may be—be it a loving parent, genuine teacher, or wise and respected religious figure. After all, it is our experience and understanding of reality that will really matter to us, not another's.

To really discover and experience things for ourselves we need to look at things in a new way, observe them with clarity, curiosity, sincerity, honesty, and openness, and do our best not to allow our personal biases, beliefs and opinions to interfere. We need to be able to observe ourselves in a similar manner, and look at the beliefs that shape our worldview, see how they were formed, how they affect us, and most importantly, see whether they are true or not.

Everything that we perceive passes through a layer of filters before it reaches our conscious awareness—filters such as thoughts, images, sensations, memories, feelings, and beliefs—and since each of us have different thoughts, imagination, sensations, memories, feelings, and beliefs, each of us interpret our experiences uniquely. It is not difficult to see that the differences in our internal filters shape our perception of the external world. But what is more difficult to see is exactly what these filters are, where they come from and exactly how they influence us.

The Merriam-Webster Dictionary definition of belief is: *something that is accepted, considered to be true, or held as an opinion.* The definition for perception is: *the way you think about or understand someone or something.* Can you see how our beliefs play a role in how we perceive things? Whatever we *consider or accept to be true* determines *the way that we think about or understand* reality. Our beliefs govern our perception, causing us to limit our experience only to what we personally believe to be true, filtering out or preventing us from experiencing everything that does not align with our personal beliefs.

Beliefs cause us to distort reality so that it fits within the model our minds have created to define reality. A perfect example of this is when a referee makes a call in a football game. It's not uncommon for the fan of one team to be pleased with the call, while another is upset with it. Both fans experienced the same event, but both were operating under different beliefs and personal biases of what was fair and unfair.

Whether we feel that something is fair or unfair, good or bad, pleasant or unpleasant, etc. has much to do with our biases and personal beliefs. Our beliefs shape the reality that we experience. Unfortunately, most people never question their perceptions or their experience, and so, rarely ever do they inquire into the source of their beliefs.

So where do our beliefs come from? Some of them you created yourself based on your personal experiences and observations of the world. They started out as assumptions about how parts of the world are, but over time they became hardened expectations which act like a lens and filter through which you view and interpret the world.

While we do create some of our beliefs ourselves, most of our beliefs have simply been adopted from others or were impressed upon us by society. We all absorb our culture's norms, but we often fail to acknowledge what these are, and investigate whether these norms are serving us or limiting us. The truth is, many of the beliefs that we adopt are disempowering and counterproductive, and we don't even know it. Also, most of our beliefs are subconscious, meaning they operate without our conscious awareness of them, making them difficult to detect, but even more influential on our perception and behavior.

The way that we take on beliefs from society is typically through imitation and conditioning. We are all born into a culture that has a certain story, and as we grow, we too begin living that story and carrying it on. During childhood, we become indoctrinated by authority figures such as parents, teachers, priests, experts, etc. We are also heavily influenced by our peers and by the type of media we are exposed to, the type of movies we watch, and the type of music we listen to.

One of the psychological factors that encourages our adoption of beliefs offered by society is our deep-rooted need to fit in and be accepted. Because of this, there is a very strong bias to conform to both the beliefs and behaviors of our society. Often the desire to belong is much stronger than the desire to do what is right, causing people to override their personal opinions and moral judgment for the sake of feeling accepted.

What makes this process even worse is that we often become strongly identified with, and attached to our beliefs, regardless of their source. And for better or worse, we'll even stubbornly defend these beliefs and unwittingly pass them on to others, including our children.

However, it is important to note that your beliefs govern how you think and act, but they are not you. You can change your beliefs, and thus change your experience and understanding of reality, but to do this, it is helpful to inquire into your beliefs and understand their origin.

I want to invite you to take an honest look at your beliefs, and the beliefs of our culture, because if you can really look at them objectively, you will see that it is our beliefs that make us suffer. Many people hold onto beliefs that limit them and cause them harm—beliefs that they aren't worthy, aren't capable, aren't good enough, etc. They carry these beliefs with them in their hearts and minds and let them influence their entire lives.

Imagine all the unnecessary pain and suffering that comes simply from limiting and false beliefs. Wouldn't you want to know if you were carrying a belief that caused you pain, a belief that made you see the world in a way that simply wasn't true? Wouldn't you want to be free of this belief, and see the world in a way that was in harmony with reality, and that brought you joy rather than suffering?

Nearly everyone carries layer upon layer of beliefs that limit them, and are so deeply engrossed in these beliefs that they aren't even aware of them, and do not have the space to really see them for what they are.

It is our beliefs that cause us to view reality in a certain way, and thus experience it accordingly. This is happening on an individual level, but it is also happening as a society. To observe your beliefs, to inquire into them and to question them is the only way to become free of them.

Do you know your beliefs about life? Do you know where they come from? Have you ever questioned them? As mentioned before, most of our beliefs come from our society, and so, I would like to inquire with you into the dominant beliefs of our culture, and become aware of how these beliefs have shaped our lives, both as individuals, and as a collective. Most importantly, I would like for us to genuinely ask whether these beliefs are accurate descriptions of reality, and if they are serving us or limiting us.

Before we inquire into these cultural beliefs, it is important to be aware of a roadblock that we might face on this journey of inquiry. There is a common term in psychology known as Cognitive Dissonance. Cognitive dissonance refers to a situation involving conflicting attitudes, beliefs or behaviors, which produces a feeling of discomfort, leading to an alteration in one of the attitudes, beliefs or behaviors to reduce the discomfort and restore balance.

Basically, cognitive dissonance is a psychological term used to explain the phenomenon that when people are confronted with information that opposes the beliefs that they strongly identify with, people will ignore, resist, or alter the information in order to maintain the validity of their belief. People often feel security in their beliefs, and when these beliefs are challenged, it can make people feel very insecure and uncertain, causing them to push away this challenging information so that they can feel safe and comfortable again.

This happens very often, and it is the reason why people typically choose to ignore or justify their belief, rather than changing their behavior when confronted with something that challenges their belief. I want you to be aware of this phenomenon, because we are going to inquire into the beliefs of our culture together, and this will require you to inquire into your personal beliefs as well.

I want you to keep in mind that I am not trying to offend anyone with this inquiry, nor am I trying to force any new belief upon you or convince you into accepting anything that I say. I am only asking you to inquire into your beliefs and to honestly ask yourself whether they are true or not. What you choose to believe in and whether you choose to be honest in your inquiry is completely up to you.

JOSEPH P. KAUFFMAN

2   CULTURAL MODELS

*"The first thing that we have to do is to get our perspectives
with some background, about the basic ideas, which as
westerners living today, influence our everyday common sense—
our fundamental notions about what life is about—and there
are historical origins for this, which influence us more strongly
than most people realize; ideas of the world which are built into
the very nature of the language we use, and of our ideas of logic,
and of what makes sense all together."*

—*Alan Watts*

Every culture has a narrative that they live by, some
kind of model that describes the Universe, and provides a
framework for understanding oneself and one's place in
the world. This narrative is the myth of our culture, the
image with which we try to understand and describe

reality. You can imagine just how influential a cultural narrative is, as it literally determines who people believe themselves to be, how people relate to the world, and how people interact with the world. Thus, the way a society behaves is very much a reflection of who they believe themselves to be.

Our culture currently operates under the influence of two very powerful images, images that we can refer to as the two basic models of the universe. The first model can be labeled as the model of "world-as-artifact." An artifact is something that is made, and likewise, this model of the universe operates under the assumption that the world is also something that was made. The "world-as-artifact" model of the universe is based on the book of Genesis, from which Judaism, Islam, and Christianity, derive their basic picture of the world. The image of the world in the book of Genesis is that the world is an artifact, something that was crafted and made by the hands of God, just as a potter takes clay and forms a pot out of it.

This model of the world sees God as the great architect, who has in mind a plan, and who fashions the universe according to that plan. The basic premise of this worldview is that the universe is made of stuff, of matter, and with this matter, the potter shapes the world with it according to his plan.

In the book of Genesis, the Lord God creates Adam out of the dust of the Earth, and breathes life into him, and in this way, we have also inherited a conception of ourselves, as being artifacts, as being made.

Interestingly, this model of the universe originated in cultures where the form of government was monarchical, and therefore, the maker of the universe was conceived also at the same time in the image of the king of the universe. And so, all of those who are oriented to the universe in this way, feel related to reality as though they are under the rule of a king, and must behave according to the rules of the kingdom or risk punishment. We have an idea that the lord of the universe must be respected in a certain way—people kneel, people bow, people prostrate themselves, etc. People often fear God, and throughout history religious authorities have taken advantage of this fear and have used it as a way to influence and control the minds of the public.

Because of this corruption and desire for power, the Church became an organization of control, and so, naturally, many humans revolted against the church and other organized religions in an attempt to reclaim their sovereignty.

This lead many people to favor the second model of the universe, which is the model of "world-as-machine." In this model, rather than the world being a creation of God, it has become somewhat of a mechanical process, unfolding randomly, with no purpose whatsoever.

The primary influences of the model of "world-as-machine" stem from three revolutions: The Scientific Revolution, and the two Industrial Revolutions of the eighteenth and nineteenth century, which transformed the cultural conditions of the West into the developed world we know today.

During the scientific revolution, scientists believed that they could make sense of the world by studying its individual components. With the publication of the *Philosophiae Naturalis Principa Mathematica* (Mathematical Principles of Natural Philosophy) in 1687, Sir Isaac Newton, the father of modern physics, described a universe in which all matter was thought to move according to fixed laws within three-dimensional time and geometric space.

Newton depicted a universe in which things existed independently from each other, complete in themselves, with their own individual boundaries. This lead us to believe that we were limited to our physical bodies, and that we ended with the outer layer of our skin, at which point the rest of the universe begins. This belief was further enhanced by the French philosopher Rene Descartes, when he wrote of man's essential separation from his universe in a philosophy that banished any kind of holistic intelligence from nature and portrayed matter as being purely mechanistic.

The Newtonian paradigm of nature-as-machine was further reinforced by the invention of the most influential machine of all: the steam engine. Steam and the development of machine tools not only affected the production of food, fuel, heating, manufacturing, and transport; they also profoundly affected human beings by separating them from the natural world.

In every way life was broken down into systematic sequences. Work was ordered by an assembly line, and workers became one more cog in the wheel of production. Time was parceled in hours and minutes, and not through the seasons of planting and harvest. The large number of people working in assembly lines no longer followed the rhythms of nature, but followed the rhythms of machines.

The second industrial revolution in the nineteenth century then introduced modern technology with the advent of steel and petroleum manufacturing and led to the rise of the middle class, which in turn paved the way for modern capitalism and the promotion of the individual and his interests.

We can see that through the influences of these historic events, our understanding of nature has slowly been transformed into a vast machine, and that we, as living beings, were completely out of place in this mechanistic universe, leaving us to feel anything but at home in nature.

While these historic events drastically shaped our cultural beliefs and ways of living, the scientific discovery with the most prevalent hand in our worldview is Charles Darwin's theory of evolution through natural selection. Darwin, a naturalist and biologist, spent many years studying nature, and concluded that there were not enough resources to allow all of life to thrive, and so, life must evolve through what he termed a "struggle for existence."

After reading Darwin's book *"The Origin of Species,"* British philosopher Herbert Spencer coined the famous term "survival of the fittest," and with some convincing, Darwin adopted the term. This became very popular in the world of business, as it provided a philosophy to justify overly competitive and greedy behavior. According to the "survival of the fittest" narrative, an individual or population thrives only at another's expense. It was this belief that provided the notion of a dog-eat-dog world, a zero sum game where selfishness and greed became the motives for success.

Today the focus is mainly on Darwin's book *The Origin of Species*. But in the 828-page sequel in which he tells us will now deal with human evolution, *The Descent of Man*, Darwin writes only twice of "survival of the fittest," but 95 times of love. He writes of selfishness only 12 times, but 92 times of moral sensitivity. He writes of competition 9 times, but 24 times of mutuality and mutual aid.

What Darwin actually believed has been twisted by a century of economic, political, and scientific interests to promote the exact opposite of his original intention. Despite Darwin's liberal use of the term "survival of the fittest," almost immediately the narrower meaning of the metaphor stuck, offering a scientific framework for all the various growing social and economic movements of the day. Most subsequent interpretations of Darwin's work, even in his lifetime, promoted a vision of all aspects of life as a battle over scarce resources, in which only the toughest and most single-minded survived.

The English biologist Thomas Huxley significantly extended this view of a dog-eat-dog world in his belief that it was responsible for the evolution of culture, ideas, and even the human mind. Huxley was convinced that it was the natural order for human beings to put their own interests above all others, and thanks to newly invented telegraphic cables and developments in print making, this destructive misinterpretation of Darwin's theory quickly swept across the world.

As a result of these major historical events, for more than three hundred years our worldview has been shaped by a story that describes us as isolated beings competing for survival on a lonely planet in an indifferent universe. Life as defined by modern science is essentially predatory, self-serving, and solitary. This is the dominant worldview of our culture. This is what most people believe to be true, whether they are conscious of it or not, and it is from this belief that people act in the world. But where has this belief left us?

JOSEPH P. KAUFFMAN

3   THE WOUND OF SEPARATION

*"The greatest illusion of this world is the illusion of
separation. Things you think are separate and different are
actually one and the same. We are all one people. But we live
as if divided."*

—*Guru Pathik*

The accepted worldview of our culture has lead us all
to believe that we are isolated beings, who exist
independently from nature and from those around us. We
see ourselves as strangers in the Universe. We feel alien, as
if we do not belong here.

Because we feel ourselves to be separate from the
world in which we live, we also feel very alone in this
world. Our sense of loneliness and isolation not only
makes us feel miserable, but it also causes us to be anxious

and afraid of the world and everyone in it. Because of this inherent fear, we put up all kinds of barriers to protect us from the world—barriers that we have created to keep us safe, but really end up making us feel more alone, more miserable, and more afraid, as they prevent us from being our natural selves.

These protective barriers are constantly trying to prevent us from feeling hurt, feeling embarrassed, feeling harm from any form of danger—but they also prevent us from opening up to others, from relating to others and being vulnerable with others. These barriers that were put in place for protection, really only divide us further from each other, and make us feel imprisoned by our own fears.

Along with the protective barriers that we put up comes a desire to further ensure our protection by glorifying our self-image in an attempt to fit in and feel accepted by others. We invest far too much time and energy in trying to impress other people, worrying about whether they will judge us or not, and even judging ourselves according to their standards. We have confused our true identity with our social image, and because we no longer know who we are, we depend on the survival and strength of this image for our own feelings of acceptance and worth.

We believe ourselves to be disconnected from the totality of nature, and this has produced a deep feeling of lack in our lives, causing us to endlessly search for happiness in objects, experiences, and people to fill the emptiness and make us feel whole again. We crave pleasure, material riches, and stimulating experiences—anything that will distract us from this inherent lack of connection. But this sense of lack comes from our sense of feeling separate from the Whole, and it will only be changed when we realize our essential oneness.

It is because we feel that we are separate from nature that we also feel it is okay to manipulate it, pollute it, and cause it harm. We project our inner turmoil onto the planet, causing outer turmoil. Nearly all of the disasters of our time—war, famine, oppression, social injustice, environmental pollution, extinction—arise from this delusional belief that we have an existence independent of the world we live in.

Believing that we are separate from one another causes us to fight against one another, and feel the need to protect ourselves from those we see as threats. Believing we are separate causes us to ignore the poverty and injustice in the world, and neglect those in need. Believing we are separate causes us to focus only on those things that benefit our own lives and those with whom we are familiar. Believing that we are separate makes us feel okay with polluting or destroying the environment, because we don't see it as directly affecting us.

All of this misery in the world, all of this destruction, all of this pain and suffering—has its origins in our shared belief that we are separate beings competing for survival in a lonely and frightening universe.

4   THE NEED FOR A NEW MODEL

It is not difficult to see that the cause of our suffering is this belief in our separation. This belief is deeply ingrained in the human mind, and it is from this belief that all of our actions stem. If we are to ever put an end to the destruction we are doing to our planet, we will need to change the way that we relate to the planet. If we see the planet as a part of ourselves, then it will always be in our best interest to care for it and make sure it is well. To change the state of our world we need to change our beliefs about the world and our place in it.

The models of *world-as-artifact* and *world-as-machine* do not serve our species or the planet. If we wish to live on this planet for much longer, we will need to adopt a new model of the universe and our place in it, one that understands our connection to all things, and realizes the influence that all things have on one another.

As Buckminster Fuller said, *"You never change things by fighting against the existing reality. To change something, build a new model that makes the old model obsolete."* This is what I would like to do with you—create a new model of the universe, a model that benefits all beings and makes the old models of separation, greed, and competition obsolete. A model that does not limit us, but allows us to thrive. A model that does not divide us, but unites us. A model that does not lead us to live in fear, but that inspires us to live in love.

The model I propose is not *world-as-artifact* or *world-as-machine*. It is *world-as-self.* It is a model that recognizes our essential unity with all things, and understands that all beings are a part of a unified whole. The whole of the Universe is our self, and in this wholeness, all beings are one. Lao Tzu, the ancient sage attributed to writing the *Tao Te Ching,* summed it up effortlessly when he said, *"Love the world as yourself; then you can care for all things."*

If we adopted this worldview, and saw all beings as our self, we would always treat life with care, compassion, and respect. We would not cause harm to anyone, because that would be harming ourselves. We would not pollute or destroy nature, because that would be polluting and destroying ourselves. All of our actions would be considerate of every living being, and would naturally be aimed at benefiting all beings, because that is what would be of most benefit to ourselves.

I hope you can see how this simple shift in perception could be the solution to the problems that humanity faces. I believe that it is the solution, and by adopting this model as my own way of viewing the world, every area of my life has changed. When I buy something at the store, I now care about how it was produced and if anything was harmed in the process. When I eat food, I now only eat things that were grown sustainably and do not harm the planet with toxic chemicals and fertilizers. When I interact with other living beings I see them as myself, and am naturally able to have compassion for them, and to overlook any negative or unconscious behaviors. Really my whole life has changed from this realization of our unity.

How can I harm someone when I realize that person is myself? How could I steal from someone when I know that I am just stealing from myself? How can I destroy something when I understand that I am destroying myself? With this understanding of oneness at the root of all our actions, there is no way we can cause harm, as all of our actions are focused on what is of most benefit for all beings.

This might sound impractical or farfetched to some, but I assure you it is not. It is the most practical and sane worldview that we could adopt, because it is a worldview that reflects the truth of our oneness. We are all connected and we are all dependent upon this planet for our existence. I believe the realization of our oneness is the only thing that can really make a difference in healing the state of our world as it currently is.

But to adopt this worldview, one has to realize it for oneself. It has to be true for you and your own experience. To base it merely on intellectual belief is shallow, and won't uproot the deeper belief of separation that has been instilled in us for hundreds of years.

You have to inquire into it, see the logic in it, contemplate it, reflect on it, and meditate on it, until you feel deep in your heart that this is true. Only then will it be strong enough to motivate and direct your actions.

The suffering that comes from a worldview based on separation is something we are all familiar with, because it is something we have all been through being raised in this culture. Almost all of our personal and collective suffering stems from our belief in separation. But the reality of nature is that nothing is separate, so we have been suffering as an entire society from a belief that simply isn't true.

5   INTERBEING

"We are not just a skin-encapsulated ego, a soul encased in flesh. We are each other and we are the world."
— *Charles Eisenstein*

Without making any changes to the materialist paradigm based on Newtonian physics, we can still see that a worldview of separation is largely untrue. We are inextricably bound to everything in nature, and looking deeply, we cannot really find where one "thing" ends and another begins.

Naturalist John Muir put it perfectly when he said, *"When we try to pick out anything by itself, we find it hitched to everything else in the Universe."* Let's look at our bodies for example. Our bodies are typically believed to be separate from nature, or at least that is how most people feel, but what is it that sustains this body?

Every day we eat food from the earth, drink water from the rivers and streams, depend on the heat from the sun, breathe the air from the sky—we couldn't last very long without food, without water we couldn't last even a week, without heat we would be dead in hours, and without air we could not survive for even a few minutes.

You can see just how dependent we are on the elements for our survival, and it is something that all of us have in common. We are all connected through these elements, and we all depend on them for physical life.

As obvious as this is, it is something we tend to overlook in our day to day lives. Even in something as simple as our morning meal we can see the whole Universe supporting our existence. There is the food that we are eating, cultivated by farmers, grown in the soil, watered by the rain, fed by the sunlight, existing in the field of space which holds together all things. The entire universe is present in every meal we eat, every breath we take, and every cell of our being. Buddhist monk Thich Nhat Hanh explained this well when he said:

"The concept of "person," like the concept of self, is made only of nonperson elements—sun, clouds, wheat, space, and so on. Thanks to these elements there is something we call a person. But erecting a barrier between the idea of person and the idea of non-person is erroneous."

There is a Buddhist philosophy called *Shunyata*, or *Emptiness* in English, which points out the interdependence of all things, or our "interbeing" as Thich Nhat Hanh commonly describes it. Buddhist philosophy points out that nothing has an independent existence, but that all things depend on one another for their existence. This is why it is called "Emptiness," because all things are empty of any inherent existence—inherent meaning fixed, unchanged, or complete in itself.

Take a flower for example. We look at something called "flower" as if it is something that exists inherently as its own entity. But when we look beyond the surface, we see that the flower is made of petals, a stem, and roots— none of which contain the "flower" as we know it.

Likewise, each one of these parts are the sum of even smaller parts. A petal, for example, is made of different tissues, which are made of cells, which are made of molecules, which are made of atoms, etc.

Nothing exists in itself, but is dependent upon the different things that make it.

A tree is made of a trunk, branches, leaves, and roots, which depend upon the soil, the sun, the rain, the clouds, etc. Deconstructing any "thing" in the Universe, we see that the whole of nature is connected to this one object.

We are no different. Our bodies are made of organs and tissues, which are made of cells, composed of molecules, which come from atoms that originated billions of years ago. Each one of our bodies are connected to the entire Universe, and are made of elements as old as stars.

Nothing in the world is separate, and as we have seen, there is really no such thing as a "thing." Because in order for anything to exist, it must be distinguished from everything else. If no distinction is made between a specific thing and everything else, then there is only an undifferentiated everything.

We are like waves in the ocean, which appear to be separate on the surface, but are in reality connected to the ocean as whole. In fact, a wave is a movement and expression of the entire ocean. Likewise, we are more than just a part of the whole Universe. We are the whole

Universe expressing itself as an individual part. What a miracle!

"You are not IN the universe, you ARE the universe, an intrinsic part of it.

Ultimately you are not a person, but a focal point where the universe is becoming conscious of itself."

—*Eckhart Tolle*

JOSEPH P. KAUFFMAN

6   THE MYSTERY OF CONSCIOUSNESS

"Consciousness cannot be accounted for in physical terms. For consciousness is absolutely fundamental. It cannot be accounted for in terms of anything else."
— Erwin Schrödinger, Nobel-Prize Winning Physicist

As we have seen, even through the lens of our modern, materialistic paradigm we can see that nothing is separate, and that all things interconnect and influence one another. All things are one with the whole of nature. Yet, the materialistic paradigm is still limited, in that it does not account for the existence of consciousness.

Our current paradigm sees the universe as a type of machine, and this does not explain how a living being—a conscious, experiencing entity—comes to be in this universe. Our mechanistic worldview cannot explain anything about our existence beyond the realm of our physical bodies.

Our world culture is founded on the belief that reality consists of two essential ingredients: mind and matter. In this duality, matter is seen as the primary element, giving rise to the current paradigm in which it is believed that somehow mind, or consciousness, is derived from matter.

While this is the primary belief of our culture, there is no scientific evidence to prove that this is so. It is believed that consciousness is a product of the brain, but no one can locate where in the brain consciousness originates. In science, this is known as the "hard problem of consciousness." Yet even though there is no evidence to prove consciousness is a product of the brain, most scientists still hold the firm conviction that this is so.

In reality, consciousness remains a mystery. As mysterious as it is, it is the fundamental ground of all experience. Without consciousness, there can be no experience. Consciousness is the element of yourself that is observing these words, it is the screen on which all experience is happening, it is your essential, observing self.

Scientists have trouble learning about consciousness because they are trying to observe it as something outside of themselves. This is impossible however, as consciousness cannot be observed—it is the awareness that is observing. It is our innermost self. To observe the observer is like trying to touch the tip of your finger with the same finger, to cut a knife with its own blade, or burn fire with its own flame—it cannot be done.

You cannot make an object out of your own subjective experience. It is not something you can separate yourself from or stand outside of to observe. It is something you have to study within yourself, as yourself, which is why the ancient sages and mystics of the east always guided us to look within to understand the truth of who we are.

Science has always tried to be as objective as possible in its observations, and to refrain from any interference of subjective experience. This has proven successful for many studies in the past, but when it comes to studying experience itself we run into an unavoidable truth—that ultimately, all experience *is* subjective. Therefore, it is not subjective experience that should be rejected in scientific inquiry, but rather personal, or exclusive experience.

JOSEPH P. KAUFFMAN

Some philosophers even go as far as rejecting consciousness itself, claiming it to be an illusion of chemical activity in the brain. In doing so, they deny the most substantial element of experience—consciousness itself—and proclaim the existence of a substance known as "matter" which is proving to be less and less substantial the more it is studied.

Scientists have discovered that every particle of what we call matter, is composed of 99.9999999999999% empty space—revealing that solid matter makes up very little of this universe, regardless of what we may perceive. In fact, modern scientists are beginning to discover that the very existence of matter is dependent upon the existence of consciousness. Revolutionary physicist Max Planck, the originator of quantum theory, once stated that:

"All matter originates and exists only by virtue of a force which brings the particle of an atom to vibration and holds this most minute solar system of the atom together.

We must assume behind this force the existence of a conscious and intelligent mind.

This mind is the matrix of all matter."

Planck regarded consciousness as the fundamental substance of the Universe, and regarded matter as derivative from consciousness. He was also aware of the issue in trying to observe consciousness through the common methods of scientific observation when he stated that, *"Science cannot solve the ultimate mystery of nature. And that is because, in the last analysis, we ourselves are a part of the mystery that we are trying to solve."*

Max Planck is not the only physicist to claim consciousness as the fundamental reality. Thomas Young, Erwin Schrodinger, Amit Goswami, Fred Alan Wolf, and numerous other well-respected physicists have discovered the same thing. These are people that have dedicated their entire lives to studying the nature of existence—studying the very fabric of what makes up our universe—and they are claiming that energy only exists as a particle of matter when it is being observed, otherwise it exists as a wave-form in a field of quantum potential.

As radical and farfetched of a statement as this may seem, there is scientific evidence to support these discoveries such as the "Double-Slit Experiment," the "Delayed Choice Quantum Eraser Experiment," the famous thought-experiment of "Schrodinger's Cat," among others. The physicists that study reality at the quantum scale, and conduct these experiments, are simply sharing what the experiments reveal—as shocking as they may be. New discoveries in this field of science are completely shifting the way we view reality, and the way we view ourselves, and the old paradigm of believing ourselves to be insignificant creatures in a random and mechanical universe is beginning to fall apart.

Matter is not the fundamental substance of existence—Consciousness is. We, as consciousness, are the most substantial element of all existence, for in our truest sense, we are existence itself. Mystics and meditators have known this since ancient times—discovering the truth of reality by looking deeply within themselves. They discovered that at the very source of their being is pure consciousness, and that this is the source of everything in the Universe.

"We live in illusion and the appearance of things.

There is a reality. We are that reality.

When you understand this, you see that you are nothing, and being nothing, you are everything. That is all."

—Kalu Rinpoche, Tibetan Buddhist Lama

The discovery that Consciousness is the fundamental substance of existence is something that has completely changed our understanding of ourselves and our reality. Not only does it raise some serious questions about the nature of reality, it makes the current paradigm completely obsolete. If consciousness is not dependent upon matter, but rather matter arises from consciousness, what does this say about ourselves and the reality we experience?

Can you see how this discovery radically changes everything we thought we knew about reality? Yet this is what modern science is beginning to reveal, and what the great sages and mystics have said for thousands of years. But what does our own experience tell us?

"The universe seems to be nearer to a great thought than a great machine.

It may well be… that each individual consciousness ought to be compared to a brain cell in a universal mind."

—James Jeans, English physicist, astronomer and mathematician.

7   EXPERIENCE

"It is impossible to experience the appearance of awareness. We are that awareness to which such an appearance would occur. We have no experience of a beginning to the awareness that is seeing these words. We have no experience of its birth. We have no experience that we, awareness, are born. Likewise, in order to claim legitimately that awareness dies, something would have to be present to experience its disappearance. Have we ever experienced the disappearance of awareness? If we think the answer is, 'Yes', then what is it that is present and aware to experience the apparent disappearance of awareness? Whatever that is must be aware and present. It must be awareness."

—Rupert Spira

All that is known, or could ever be known, is experience. Regardless of how we may feel about that statement, we cannot rightfully deny it. And all that is known of experience is mind—meaning that all we experience are thoughts, images, memories, feelings, sensations, sights, sounds, tastes, and smells. What appears to be external is really being experienced internally.

Take these words for example. You are reading them in what appears to be a book outside of you, yet it is being experienced on the screen of your awareness. Really, this book is something that is happening within you. Even modern science has shown that light enters the cornea, passes through the pupil, is focused on the retina, which then sends information along the optic nerve to the visual cortex located in the back of your brain. All of our sense organs (eyes, ears, nose, tongue, skin) only take in vibrations of energy and send that information to be processed by our brains. Everything you experience "out there" is occurring within your own mind.

Some philosophers theorize that there isn't really a reality "out there" to perceive, but rather that reality is something that is projected within our consciousness, and since each individual consciousness is a part of the universal consciousness, we are projecting our individual realities, which in turn create our collective reality.

This is similar to the beliefs that the Ancient Toltecs of Mexico had about reality. They believed that every being is living in their personal dream, and that together, these personal dreams create "the dream of the planet."

While our world culture operates on the belief that there is indeed a reality that exists independently of us, our experience could never verify this. Only belief could say that this is so. Therefore, if all that could ever be known is experience, and all experience is known in the form of mind, then in order to know the nature of reality, we must understand the nature of mind. Any mind that wishes to know the nature of reality, must investigate and know the reality of itself.

Everything that is known is known through the medium of mind, and whatever is perceived through the medium of mind first passes through a layer of filters—such as conditioned beliefs, opinions, memories, interests, likes and dislikes, etc.—and so, all of our knowledge and experiences are reflections of our minds' limitations.

We all have experience, but what is it that knows experience? Who or what is it that is experiencing? Who is aware of these words? Who is it that cannot be seen, but through which all seeing happens? What is it that cannot be heard, but through which all hearing happens? What is it that cannot be experienced, but through which all experience happens?

What is the most fundamental element of all experience? Our experience changes constantly, but what is the substance of experience? What is the screen on which experience is playing? With what is all experience known? A thought cannot know an emotion, an emotion cannot know a sensation, a sensation cannot know a perception. These things are known or experienced, they do not know or experience. Whatever it is that knows experience, cannot be directly experienced, for it is the substance of experience.

Can you find within yourself that irreducible substance? What is the part of you that is you, the true you, not something that appears to exist outside of you—not your body, your name, your job, your education, your culture, your beliefs, your emotions, your personality, or your thoughts. These are all things that exist apart from the true you, which is why we always refer to them as "my body," "my name," "my job," "my thoughts," etc. What is this "my" or "I" that we are referring to? The common name we give to the knowing or experiencing element of mind is "I," but what is the nature of this "I"?

"I" am that which knows all experience, but am not myself an experience. "I" am that which is aware of thoughts, feelings, and sensations, but "I" myself am not a thought, feeling, or sensation. Whatever the content of my experience, "I" am the one who experiences it. Thus, awareness is the common factor in all experience.

Everything that we experience is changing constantly. Our body changes, our mind changes, our personality changes, our likes and dislikes change, careers change, friends change, circumstances change. But awareness itself does not change. Consciousness is the continuous element that underlies all experience.

Have you not felt like you are the same person you have always been throughout your life? While all of the cells that make your body are constantly changing, as is your personality, the thoughts in your mind, the interests you have, and the circumstances you experience, there is a part of you that feels continuous, a part of you that is a constant, a part that remains unchanged.

What is this part of you that is not altered by changing circumstances? What is that part of you that cannot change because it has no form? It is awareness itself—pure consciousness, pure knowing, pure being. Without you as the substance of all experience, what is there to experience? Who would be experiencing it? Can you see how the requirement for any experience is you—the one who is experiencing?

This knowing awareness is the common element in all experience. It is the element of experience that is shared by all living beings, regardless of species, race, color, gender, culture, or social class. All living beings are aware, and this is true under all circumstances, and in all situations. Consciousness is what unites us all. At the very source of our being lies pure awareness—the fundamental substance of existence.

8   THE SELF

"As you watch your mind, you discover your self as the watcher. When you stand motionless, only watching, you discover your self as the light behind the watcher. The source of light is dark, unknown is the source of knowledge. That source alone is. Go back to that source and abide there."

—*Sri Nisargadatta Maharaj*

I would like to ask you to participate in a small experiment. After this paragraph, take a few minutes to simply sit and observe your thoughts. Just sit, close your eyes, and observe whatever arises in the field of your awareness. When thoughts come, don't try to make sense of them or feed them with more thoughts, just witness them, and allow them to come and go as they please. Try to feel the presence that precedes the thoughts. Recognize that you are not your thoughts, but that you are the witness of thought. Try this experiment for yourself and see if this is true for you.

~~~

If you participated in this small experiment, you probably noticed that it is rather difficult to remain in a state of pure, passive observation without being distracted by the thoughts and sensations that arise. But if you are capable of sustaining a period of time simply observing without thinking, then you will also notice that when your thoughts are gone, you are still there. Even if you cannot stop your thoughts on command, moments come when naturally you are not thinking anything, and during these moments are you not still there? Are you able to notice yourself as distinct from your thoughts, as the observer of thought, or the awareness in which thought exists?

The following passage is an excerpt from my book, *"The Answer is YOU."* I have inserted it again here because it is relevant to the topic being discussed:

"In the Hindu tradition, your witnessing consciousness is referred to as the Self. However, this is just a name, and no name can truly describe the pure essence of consciousness that is YOU. But you can still feel this essence that is you, even if you cannot accurately define it. Simply by trying to define or label ourselves we only limit ourselves to that label, and a label is not who we are. No label can define the immensity of your true nature. You are the awareness that precedes every label, the awareness that is perceiving these words and turning them into thoughts, the awareness that creates the world with every act of observation.

You cannot be aware of yourself, for you are awareness itself. How can a witness witness itself? That is like trying to see your own eyes without a reflection, or cut a knife with the tip of its own blade—it is impossible. The subject can only observe the object; it cannot make an object out of itself. But by the very act of observing you indirectly know yourself as the observer, as the subject. No witnessing of the witness is needed to prove its existence.

This is the dilemma that modern science has when it tries to come up with a definition for consciousness. The modern scientist attempts to step outside of himself in order to observe himself, an attempt that is always doomed for failure. You cannot make an object out of your subjective experience, but you know that consciousness exists, simply because you exist.

Being, in itself, is proof of your existence, so it is also quite clear that you are not nothing, otherwise who would be there to know that they are nothing? Only one who exists can say "I don't exist." To be aware of the world, of nothingness, or of anything at all, you first have to be. This essential state of Being is who you are, only you have forgotten who you are because you have been

63

lead away from your source. You have lost touch with your true nature by being raised and conditioned in a society in which everyone else is also out of touch with their true nature.

Think about why it is so difficult to know who you really are. If you could be your name, your body, or your position in society, then the question would be easy to answer. If you were something that had a form, with a certain characteristic or quality, then you would actually be that form and there would be no uncertainty about it. But consciousness is something that exists outside of space, outside of time, and thus is without form. This is the reason why your observing consciousness often goes unnoticed, even though it is always there, and you are always it. It is no thing— no object with form, but just simply, undeniably, you.

This witnessing consciousness, this formless dimension of yourself, is the awareness in which your experience happens, yet it remains untouched by this experience at all times. It is similar to the background of white on which you are reading these words. This white background allows any and every word to exist within it, yet it is not confined to any of these words. Similarly, your awareness allows any and every form to exist within it, but it is not bound to any of these forms.

Existing without form or quality, this consciousness also has no miserable or joyful past, no dreams or doubts about the future, no beliefs to fight over or defend, no pain or struggle to tolerate, no body to criticize or improve. When you reconnect with yourself as pure awareness, all of those just fade away, revealing themselves as things that are distinct from you.

We only suffer when we falsely identify with the objects that arise in our awareness, rather than with the awareness itself— when we identify with our thoughts, with our emotions, our personal history, and the many stories we tell ourselves. When you reconnect to your source—the essence of your being, the pure and impartial witness—you become free from all of the troubles of the material world; free from the world of form. You no longer feel the desire to cling to forms or depend on them for your happiness. Instead, you are free to enjoy form, free to let form be, and free to allow all forms to come and go as they please. All forms are impermanent and changing, but your consciousness, being formless, is eternal, and exists regardless of the forms that it gives life to.

Without form or quality what could change? How can something that has no form ever die? It can't because it was never born. It simply is. It is existence itself. In Sanskrit, this subjective experience of the ultimate, unchanging reality is described as Satchitananda *or Truth (*Sat*), Consciousness (*Chit*), Bliss (*Ananda*). Your true being, as Consciousness, is ever at peace, ever at rest, eternally existing in the dimension of here and now. It is the formless and eternal quality within you that expresses itself through the world of form.*

Since all forms are undergoing constant change, shouldn't it be obvious that the absolute and unchanging Truth of who you are must be without form? Could you imagine accomplishing anything, saying anything, or thinking anything without this formless consciousness being present? It is impossible to imagine, because how could any of the things that you do happen without someone inside of you—that is you—experiencing what is happening? Who would be there to adjust to circumstances, adapt to the environment, develop, and grow? Without consciousness, nothing can happen and nothing can be experienced. You can do things without acknowledging it or thinking about it, but it is still always present. You cannot even be unaware of it without it being there. You, as Consciousness, are essential to everything, the essence of everything, and without your witnessing, there is no reality that can be witnessed."

It is my hopes that this passage has conveyed to you the Truth of your real Self—pure awareness. It is important to understand the distinction between the true Self of pure awareness, and the illusory self of the mind— the psychological, or ego self.

Essentially, we have become heavily identified with our egos, believing ourselves to truly be this individual person, with his or her history, challenges, dreams, responsibilities, etc. And while the ego has its reality, it is not the truth of who we are. Our true nature is the awareness that observes the ego and its drama, the awareness that witnesses all of our experiences.

If we wish to reach new levels of freedom, joy, and peace, we must shift our identification with our ego self to our true self as awareness—and this is not always easy. We were born and raised to identify with our individual egos, and so it has become a habitual way of orienting ourselves in the world, a habitual way of interpreting our experiences, and a habitual way of thinking, feeling, and living.

This ego-identified way of being functions in unconscious, mechanical, behavior—as though we are operating on auto-pilot, unaware of the moment in which we are living. To awaken to our true Self, and to shift identification from our ego self, we must exercise our awareness.

Start observing yourself, your thoughts, your actions, your habitual responses, etc. The more you observe your experience, the more you realize your true nature as the observer—the observer that is ultimately never effected by the experience it is observing. Even if you are suffering greatly, the awareness that is observing this experience remains in a dimension of reality that is untouched and free. The more we shift our identification to our true nature as awareness, the less we suffer, and the more free we become.

Yet, we do not realize just how heavily identified we are with our ego self. We do not realize how unconscious we are of ourselves and of the moment in which we live. As you become more aware, you begin to realize just how unaware you have been. You start to wake up from the dream of habitual, ego-identified behavior, and you are amazed at how you allowed yourself to live in such a dream-like state for so long.

Part of the challenge of awakening from this dream is that with awareness, comes the realization of our freedom, and with this freedom, comes a sense of responsibility. We are no longer able to live in ignorance, doing things unconsciously without worrying about their effect, and this causes us to shift our behavior, and change our lifestyle. But our habits are stubborn, and we often continue repeating them, becoming more and more aware of how they are not serving us, until finally we make the decision to change the habits once and for all, which always entails some form of mental and emotional discomfort.

As the renowned psychologist Carl Jung said, *"there is no coming to consciousness without pain."* As we become more aware of life and of ourselves, we have to face things that we have been ignoring, things that have been lying dormant in our subconscious minds. We begin to notice our thoughts, how we think, what we think, and how these thoughts affect us. We begin to notice our actions, the way we act, and how these actions affect us. We begin to notice our conditioning, parts of our personality that we may not like, things that happened to us that have left an emotional scar—all of these things come up to the surface, and are presented to us so that we may heal from them, and change them to match our new understanding of reality.

As Carl Jung is also noted for saying, *"you do not become enlightened by imagining figures of light, but by making the unconscious conscious."* We wake up by bringing awareness to what has been unconsciously functioning in us, by bringing the light of consciousness into the darkness of our unconscious behavior.

Some are able to let go of their habits, change their behavior, and immediately begin living the truth of their being the moment that they realize it. Most of us, however, are not so fortunate. We have to work at it, we have to practice, we have to make an effort—to remain mindful of the present moment and how we respond to it, to heal from our emotional wounds, to unlearn our conditioning, to see through our false beliefs and to realize fully the truth of who we are, and to live this truth in our lives.

What makes this process challenging is that we are very comfortable in our ignorance and our unconscious habits, and it is difficult at times, even frightening for some, to change habits that we are so heavily identified with—

activities and modes of thinking that we associate with our very identity.

What adds to this difficulty is the fact that we live in a society which is dominated by ego and unconscious behavior. So the behavior and energy of most people around us influences us to continue living in this unconscious, egocentric way. What's more, is that when we begin living in a more mindful way, often the people around us question our behavior, or even feel threatened by it, as it challenges the way that they lead their own lives.

As we wake up, we are likely to notice things we do, that we may have no reason for why we do them, things that don't really serve us in any way. We might notice people we spend time with that actually make us miserable or weigh us down. We might notice the food we eat that is harming us, the thoughts we think that are causing us pain, the fears we have that limit our expression. All of these unconscious things become conscious, and we are called to look at them with honesty, and to change the things that do not reflect our new understanding of reality—or we may try to repress these things from coming up by falling into unconscious patterns, but this does no more than provide a momentary coping mechanism that prolongs our process of awakening.

The process of expanding our awareness always comes with it the many things we have been unconscious of, and because of this, awakening from the dream of the ego is often challenging, and many would subconsciously prefer not to do it. But this contentment in our ignorance, this way of living comfortably in our unawareness, living out a story that is untrue, and feeding a system that is broken and outdated, is the cause of all the chaos in the world, and so now more than ever each one of us has the responsibility of waking up to our true nature, so that our actions may reflect awareness and understanding, rather than ignorance and confusion.

The state of the world is pushing us to become aware of our unconscious egocentric behavior, and inviting us to awaken to the truth of our being as awareness—at the very least it is inviting us to become more aware of our actions and acknowledge the ways we impact the world.

It may be challenging to change beliefs we have identified with all our lives, and to change our understanding and definition of who we are, but it is necessary that we are willing to alter our behavior to reflect the truth of our being—the only alternative is to willingly live in ignorance of reality.

We have mistakenly identified ourselves with our thoughts, our personality, and our ego self. The ego self is the self that the mind imagines itself to be—the self that is identified with the body, that has a culture, a race, a religion, a family, a job, etc. The true Self is the spacious awareness in which this ego self operates. It is the witness of the ego's drama, not the drama itself.

The ego is the one that thinks "I am this," or "I am that," the Self is the presence that knows "I AM." You can distinguish the difference between them easily. When you are thinking "I need to accomplish this," "I want to buy that," "I should avoid this," etc.—this is really the ego self that is thinking these things. The true Self is the awareness that watches this from a place beyond the ego self.

Since the ego self is the self that is identified with the needs of the body, you could imagine that it serves a vital function in life as we currently know it. However, it is a function of the mind, and should be understood as such, for when we mistake our ego self to be who we are, and are unaware of our true Self, a life of attachment, fear and suffering is inevitable.

The great Zen master Shunryu Suzuki said, *"How much ego do you need? Just enough so that you don't step in front of a bus."* He was conveying that the ego serves a necessary function, but should be kept in its place, for if we become overly ego-identified, we become greedy, selfish, competitive, violent, are in a constant search for validation from others, seek possession and fulfillment of the mind's desires, and tend to see ourselves as better or more important than everyone else.

Another great Zen master once explained the equality of life through the game of rock, paper, scissors—in which two or more people are to simultaneously choose either, rock, paper, or scissors, each one being defeated by the next (rock is covered by paper, paper is cut by scissors, and scissors is smashed by rock). He used this simple children's game as an analogy for life, stating that nothing is stronger or weaker, but that each in turn conquers the other.

When identified with the ego however, we feel that we are more important than everyone else, and wish to either be praised or pitied because of this, neglecting the simple truth that everyone has their own experience, and so, faces many challenges and obstacles in life just as we do. We are all different and unique, and we should embrace that, but we are not separate from or superior to anyone else.

Many spiritual, philosophical and psychological teachings have different understandings and definitions of ego, and so will address the subject of ego accordingly. Some say you have to destroy the ego, to fight against it, or to erase it. However, this is more often than not something the ego believes because it thinks it will somehow improve it or make it better! As the great philosopher and self-proclaimed "spiritual entertainer," Alan Watts once said, *"the biggest ego trip going is trying to get rid of your ego."*

The way in which people speak about and deal with the ego is based on their definition and understanding of what ego is, and so a mutual agreement on these terms is necessary for having a genuine discussion about it. But regardless of the definition of ego and its qualities, it is generally understood that it is the illusory self-identity that veils the reality of our true Self. And no matter how one tries to describe the Self, all descriptions will always fall short of the reality.

This is because words are finite, and Truth is infinite. Words, by their very nature, label, limit, and divide reality, while Truth is unnamable, limitless, and undivided. To convey the infinite Truth with finite words is impossible. Every attempt to do so is doomed for failure. It is my hopes that I fail just well enough for you to get a taste of what is attempting to be conveyed, and inspire you to search deeper into this subject for yourself. For to truly know yourself as you are you have to look within yourself. You have to inquire into your own mind and find that space within you that is ever-present and free from all objective appearances, and no one can do this for you. No teacher, priest, sage, religion, film, or book can look within for you, only you can inquire into your own being.

The beautiful thing about this true Self is that you don't have to look for it anywhere outside of yourself, for it is you, and you are always present. All you have to do is quiet the mind, empty consciousness of its content, and allow it to rest as itself in the present moment. All you have to do is be as you are, and rest in your pure witnessing presence. This is the essence of all meditation, for awareness to rest in its own nature.

"Meditation is the dissolution of thoughts in Eternal awareness or Pure consciousness without objectification,

knowing without thinking, merging finitude in infinity."
— Voltaire

We will talk a bit more about meditation in a later chapter, but first I want to share with you some of the different names and definitions that have been given to the Self, to show that it has been discovered by numerous cultures from around the world, and that while all of these cultures are also subject to the limitations of language, all of them are attempting to describe the same thing.

9   ONE TRUTH, MANY TRADITIONS

"There are many traditions, but only one Great Spirit."

—Maestro Juan Gabriel

This truth of our essential Self being pure consciousness has been realized by cultures around the world, and has been known for thousands of years. It is the great secret of all traditions, the spiritual core of existence that unites us all.

I think it can be helpful to read some of the unique ways that these different cultures have attempted to define the Self, and to notice the similarities in their teachings. While much of history has been lost in the colonization of the modern world, along with much of the world's spiritual literature and accurate historical dates, the truth discovered by these cultures is timeless.

Sanatana Dharma

As far as we know, the world's most ancient religion was Sanatana Dharma, which is now popularly called Hinduism. Sanatana Dharma was the original name of the Hindu tradition, Hinduism being a term of more recent development.

The furthest we can trace this religion is to the origins of its oldest scriptures, the Vedas, the dates of which are of debate among religious scholars—some dating it back to as far as 5,000 years before the current era (BCE), over seven thousand years ago, while others say it was likely composed in 1,500 BCE, nearly four thousand years ago. Whatever the exact age of the original scriptures may be, it is said that this is only when the Vedas were written down, and that they had likely been passed down as an oral tradition for thousands of years prior to existing in written form. Thus, the true date of Sanatana Dharma's origins is unknown, however it is understood that it is a very ancient tradition.

The two words, "Sanatana Dharma," come from the ancient Sanskrit language. "*Sanatana*" is a Sanskrit word that denotes that which is *Anadi* (beginningless), *Anantha* (endless) and does not cease to be—that which is eternal and everlasting. With its profound meaning and rich connotations, *Dharma* is not translatable to any other language. Dharma comes from the Sanskrit root *dhri*, meaning to hold together, to sustain. Its approximate meaning is "Natural Law," or the principles of reality which are inherent in the very nature and design of the Universe. Thus, the term Sanatana Dharma can be roughly translated to mean *"the natural, ancient and eternal way."*

Sanatana Dharma is a code of ethics, or a way of living through which one may achieve moksha, the Sanskrit word for liberation or enlightenment. Typically, this is said to be achieved through meditation and self-inquiry, but it is essentially when awareness realizes itself as the essential substance of the Universe—which is why enlightenment is also commonly referred to as Self-realization.

What is interesting about this ancient tradition is that it is not based on the teachings of any one person, but rather was formed over time by the realizations of numerous sages and seers who spent the majority of their time in deep states of meditation. Sanatana Dharma is the philosophy that was taught by these enlightened masters.

It is a philosophy based not on belief, but on direct experience and self-inquiry. According to the ancient sages, Sanatana Dharma is the eternal law, the universal order and flow of the Universe. It was not created as a way of spreading a belief system, but rather as a way to guide those inward to discover their true Self.

Being one of the oldest of the world's religions, and having no original teacher, the teachings of Sanatana Dharma have spread to many different areas of the Indian subcontinent, and likewise have developed many different teachings and methods of attaining *moksha*, or enlightenment. As a result, it offers a great variety of descriptions for this fundamental Self of the Universe.

According to the tradition of Advaita Vedanta, the True Self is known as Atman, the "I AM" consciousness of every individual. One of their most famous sayings is that "Atman is Brahman"—Brahman being the name for the unchanging and eternal reality of the Universe. Thus, according to this tradition, the "I AM" consciousness of every individual is the unchanging and eternal reality of the Universe.

According to another Hindu tradition, Kashmir Shaivism, the ultimate reality is Shiva—pure consciousness. In this tradition, it is said that Shiva is playing a game with his beloved, Shakti (universal energy). In this game, known in Sanskrit as Lila, Shiva forgets himself in the dance with his beloved Shakti, divides himself into a multiplicity of beings, and allows himself to be enticed and entranced by Shakti's magic, only to rediscover himself as Shiva, the pure and eternal consciousness dwelling within each of the many created beings.

It is a mythical description of a cosmic game of hide and seek, in which God creates the world from his own potential, and then forgets himself in his creation, allowing him to fully experience the creation, while at the same time remaining free from it as the pure witness. According to Kashmir Shaivism, that is what is happening right now. We are all Shiva, yet we have forgotten who we really are in order to experience the joy, sorrow, and beauty of life, and are now beginning to awaken to our true nature, and remember ourselves as the primordial being of the Universe.

In Yoga, a Sanskrit word meaning union, the goal is to unite one's individual consciousness with universal consciousness. In this tradition, the realization of one's true nature as universal consciousness is called Samadhi.

Sanatana Dharma is one of the most diverse philosophies, with numerous traditions that have evolved from it. However, it is not the only tradition to speak on this universal truth.

Buddhism

There are many different forms of Buddhism, and not all of them agree with each other. Buddhism was founded on the teachings of the Buddha, a man who lived roughly 2,500 years ago. The Buddha, born Siddhartha Gautama, was born into a royal family in what is now Nepal, close to the border with India. Growing up, the Buddha was exceptionally intelligent and compassionate. Tall, strong, and handsome, the Buddha belonged to the Warrior caste.

It was predicted that he would become either a great king or spiritual leader. Since his parents wanted a powerful ruler for their kingdom, they tried to prevent Siddhartha from seeing the unsatisfactory nature of the world, and so, they surrounded him with every kind of pleasure.

He was given attractive women, sports, and entertainment of all kinds. Anything unpleasant was kept hidden from his sight, with hopes that all he would know was a world of pleasure, keeping his mind off of things that might spark his latent spiritual qualities. He was not even allowed to leave the palace, for fear that he might come upon harsh realities of the world that would have him question his existence.

However, being trapped in that palace for so long, Siddhartha grew curious, and at the age of 29, he decided to leave the palace. When he left, he was confronted with the realities of impermanence and suffering. On one of his excursions, he saw someone desperately sick. The next day, he saw a frail old man, and finally a dead person. He was very troubled to realize that old age, sickness and death were realities of life, and would eventually come to everyone he loved.

Shortly after, Siddhartha decided to leave the palace and search for a solution to the problem of suffering in life. He left behind his royal responsibilities and his family in order to search for enlightenment. He left the palace secretly, and set off alone into the forest.

Over the next six years, he met many talented meditation teachers. He studied, practiced, and mastered their techniques, but always he found that they revealed to him some of the mind's potential, but did not teach him about the nature of mind itself.

Exhausted and unsatisfied with his efforts, Siddhartha left his teachers and spiritual community, and decided to sit underneath a bodhi tree, and remain in meditation until he knew mind's true nature and could benefit all beings. After spending six days and nights cutting through the mind's most subtle obstacles, he reached enlightenment on the full moon morning of May, a week before he turned thirty-five.

At the moment of full realization, all veils of confused feelings and rigid ideas dissolved, and Siddhartha experienced the all-encompassing here and now. All separation in time and space vanished. Past, present, and future, near and far, melted into one radiant state of intuitive bliss. He became timeless, all-pervading awareness. Through every cell in his body he knew and was everything. He became *Buddha*, the Awakened One.

After his enlightenment, Buddha traveled on foot throughout northern India. He taught constantly for forty-five years. People of all castes and professions, from kings to courtesans, were drawn to him. He answered their questions, always pointing away from that which is relative and illusory, and towards that which is absolute and ultimately real.

During the time of the Buddha, the primary spiritual tradition practiced at that time was Sanatana Dharma, or Hinduism. Like all forms of organized religion, there is room for human corruption to interfere. This occurred in Hinduism in what is known as the caste-system, in which certain people are divided into different castes, some having more privileges than others.

During this time, the Brahmin caste (the caste of priests), kept all of the ancient teachings and scriptures and told the people that they could only learn these teachings through the Brahmins. The Buddha saw the injustice in the caste system, and so he rejected Hinduism, knowing that Truth was not limited to a particular tradition, religion, or caste, but that it was the birthright of all people.

The Buddha reminded us that the Truth is something we realize within ourselves, and that it is not dependent on teachers or traditions. His teachings were merely spoken to help people discover the truth for themselves, never to accept his words with blind faith.

Contrary to the teachings of Hinduism, the Buddha taught that there was no self (anatman), however his emphasis was on the self that people believe themselves to be—the ego self, or the self-identity imagined by the mind. His focus was on trying to free people from any beliefs, notions, or concepts of reality so that they could experience reality directly as it is. This direct experience of reality was said to be the state of *Nirvana*—pure awareness free from any conceptual encumbrances.

There is much debate among the different schools of Buddhism as to exactly what the Buddha taught. However, all schools agree upon the Buddha's primary teachings of the Four Noble Truths—suffering exists, there is a cause to suffering, there is a way to be free of suffering, and there is a path that leads to freedom (eightfold path). The Buddha taught that suffering was caused by ignorance of the true nature of reality, and that by realizing the true nature of reality, we attain liberation.

While not all schools of Buddhism offer a name and philosophy that resembles the Self as pure awareness, there are certainly some that do. Zen, for example, teaches that within every being there is Buddha-Nature. The teachings of Zen state that all beings are perfect as they are, that enlightenment is our natural state, and that we do not have to strive to become enlightened, but to realize our natural state we need to stop striving, because we cannot awaken to our true nature by looking for it outside of ourselves. As the famous Zen master Dogen said, *"If you cannot find the truth right where you are, where else do you expect to find it?"*

Similar to the teachings of Zen, yet originating in Tibet, the Dzogchen teachings of the Nyingma tradition suggest a comparable philosophy. According to Dzogchen, the natural state of all beings is pure, pristine, ever-present awareness—known in Tibetan as *Rigpa*. The teachings of Dzogchen assert that all beings are perfect as they are, and that all we need to do is learn to rest in our natural enlightened state.

The primary method of meditation in Dzogchen teaches the practitioner to distinguish Rigpa (pure consciousness) from the conceptual, or moving mind. The conceptual or moving mind is the familiar mind of everyday experience, constantly busy with thoughts, memories, images, internal dialogues, judgments, meanings, emotions, and fantasies. It is said that from this mind all suffering arises.

Thus, Dzogchen teaches one to be free of this mind and the suffering it causes by realizing one's true nature as Rigpa, or pure consciousness. They claim that this is both the path to liberation and liberation itself.

Dzogchen teachings often use a mirror to symbolize Rigpa. A mirror reflects everything without choice, preference, or judgement. It reflects the beautiful and the ugly, the big and the small, the virtuous and the non-virtuous. There are no limits or restrictions on what it can reflect, yet the mirror is unstained and unaffected by whatever is reflected in it. nor does it ever cease reflecting.

Similarly, all phenomena of experience arise in Rigpa: thoughts, images, emotions, the grasping and the grasped, every apparent subject and object, every experience. The conceptual mind itself arises and abides in Rigpa. Life and death take place in the nature of mind, but it is neither born nor does it die, just as reflections come and go without creating or destroying the mirror. Identifying with the conceptual mind, we live as one of the reflections of the mirror, reacting to the other reflections, suffering confusion and pain, endlessly living and dying. We take the reflections for the reality and spend our lives chasing illusions.

When the conceptual mind is free of grasping and aversion, it spontaneously relaxes into unfabricated Rigpa. Then there is no longer an identification with the reflections in the mirror and we can effortlessly accommodate all that arises in experience, appreciating every moment. If hatred arises, the mirror is filled with hatred. When love arises, the mirror is filled with love. For the mirror itself, neither love nor hatred is significant: both are equally a manifestation of its innate capacity to reflect.

This is known as the mirror-like wisdom; when we recognize the nature of mind and develop the ability to abide in it, no emotional state distracts us. Instead, all states and all phenomena, even anger, jealousy, and so on, are released into the purity and clarity that is their essence. Abiding in Rigpa, we cut karma at its root and are released from the bondage of samsara (the cycle of death and rebirth).

Taoism

Taoism is yet another tradition that offers us profound insight into the ultimate nature of reality. Taoism is a tradition based upon the teachings of the ancient book, the *"Tao Te Ching,"* which is attributed to a great sage known as *"Lao Tzu."* There is no historical evidence, however, to say whether Lao Tzu was a real person, or whether the book is really a collection of teachings from the sages of ancient China, masked under the name of *"Lao Tzu"* which translates in Chinese as *"Old Master."*

As the story goes, Lao Tzu was a wise man who lived in the city of Chengzhou (known today as Luoyang). Lao Tzu began to grow tired of the moral decay of life in Chengzhou, and predicted the kingdom's decline. He decided to venture west to live as a hermit in the unsettled frontier at the age of 80. At the western gate of the city, he was recognized by one of the guards, who, seeing this wise old man was leaving for good, asked the master to record his wisdom for the good of the country before he would be permitted to pass. The text Lao Tzu wrote was said to be the *Tao Te Ching*.

Tao has no exact English translation, but it relates most closely to the Western idea of wholeness, to the unknowable unity of the divine. Taoism emphasizes the fact that the true nature of reality is essentially unknowable. The first verse of the *Tao Te Ching*, the text attributed to Lao Tzu, states *"The Tao that can be told is not the eternal Tao. The name that can be named is not the eternal*

Name. The unnamable is the eternally real. Naming is the origin of all particular things."

Taoism points out the limits of the human mind, and says that we cannot understand the Tao with our intellectual mind, but since the Tao is present in and as all things, we can trust the natural intelligence within us, as our body's intelligence is one with the intelligence of the Universe.

Thus, one of the most common Taoist teachings is that of wu-wei, translated as non-action, or effortless action. It does not mean inaction or passivity, but activity in which there is not an "I" doing the acting, but rather we are allowing the Tao to act through us without the interference of "I" and its agenda.

Taoism is an ancient Chinese tradition that reminds us we can relax and trust nature, for we are nature, and nature is expressing itself and doing its work through us. All we have to do is flow harmoniously with the movement of nature, and all else will be taken care of.

Oneness In The West

Hinduism, Buddhism, and Taoism are very rich eastern traditions, each with various schools of thought. Each tradition, however, is founded on a common truth—the truth that all beings are one with the underlying reality of the Universe. At the core of every being lies the one Self of the Universe.

It is not only in the East that this Truth has been realized. Many western traditions have similar teachings. The great thinkers and mystics of ancient Greece had coined the term Gnosis—which means knowledge of the infinite. They believed that the world has its origins in Chaos, their term for nothingness, or the void that precedes the world. The renowned philosopher Heraclitus once stated that, "All things come out of the one and the one out of all things."

Similar to Heraclitus, all of the great philosophers of this era understood that the world possessed a type of integral unity in spite of the diversity of its appearance. Parmenides, wrote a poem titled, "On Nature," in which he claimed that the only thing we can meaningfully say of anything is that "it is." According to Parmenides, the predicate "is not" is literally nonsense: not-being is impossible, inexpressible, and inconceivable.

"That which is true must exist in eternal presence; about it cannot be said 'it was,' 'it will be.' The 'Existent' cannot have become; for out of what should it have become? Out of the 'Nonexistent'? But that does not exist and can produce nothing.

Out of the 'Existent'? This would not produce anything but
itself. The same applies to the Passing; it is just as impossible as
the Becoming, as any change, any increase, any decrease.

Thou canst not know what is not - that is impossible - nor utter
it; for it is the same thing that can be thought and that can be.

How, then, can what is to be going to be in the future? Or how
could it come into being? If it came into being, it is not; nor is it
if it is going to be in the future. Thus, is becoming extinguished
and passing away not to be heard of."

—*Parmenides 5th Century BCE*

The ancient Greek philosophers offered a fountain of wisdom to the world, but they were not the only western mystics to offer such wisdom. Rumi, a mystic from the Sufi tradition, was a very talented poet. His poems show the devotion of a true lover of truth, and serve as great pointers for those seeking a greater understanding of reality. In one of his poems, Rumi wrote, "I searched for God and found only myself. I searched for myself and found only God," illustrating the union of the individual self with the Self of the Universe. The Sufis were mystics of the Muslim tradition, in which Allah is said to be the creator of the Universe, who possesses the quality of Tawhid, or indivisible oneness.

In Judaism, this same indivisible oneness is referred to as Ein Sof, which refers to the absolute, the infinite, or that which has no end. Christians call it God. Native American tribes have often called it the Great Spirit, and claim that this Spirit lives in and through all things. The Quechua people of Peru have the term Pachakamaq, which refers to the "creator of the Universe." And in the Peruvian amazon, the Shipibo tribe has a visionary brew that they call "Uni,"—more commonly known as Ayahuasca—which according to shaman Don Jose Campos reveals that *"Consciousness never dies. It's always there... Ayahuasca takes away the masks we have and it shows you who you are."*

Taking a look at the many traditions of the world we find a common thread that unites them all. Underlying the apparent diversity and multiplicity of the world lies a fundamental unity, and this essential unity is who we really are. It is the essence of life that we all share. At the very core of experience lies universal consciousness. It is the awareness that looks through every eye, hears through every ear, tastes through every tongue, and expresses itself through every being in the Universe.

"At the center of the universe dwells the Great Spirit
And that center is really everywhere.
It is within each of us."

—*Black Elk*

10   SEEING THE SELF IN ALL

"The beginningless Consciousness is unborn, whole and, residing forever in its natural home of the Heart-cave, is without form, world or impurity. It is beyond comparison and completely unattached. It cannot be comprehended by the mind nor can it be seen or felt by the senses."

—*Ramana Maharshi*

Ramana Maharshi was one of the greatest sages in recent history. At the young age of sixteen, a sudden fear of death came over him. He was struck by "a flash of excitement," as if a "current" or "force" seemed to possess him, while his body became rigid. He initiated a process of self-inquiry, asking himself what it is that dies. He concluded that the body dies, but that this "current" or "force" remains alive, and recognized this "current" or "force" as his true Self. This realization drove him to leave behind everything he knew and flee from his home to Tiruvannamalai, where he spent the remainder of his life.

On arriving in Tiruvannamalai, Maharshi went to the temple of Arunachaleswara. The first few weeks he spent in the thousand-pillared hall, then shifted to other spots in the temple, and eventually to the *Patala-lingam* vault so that he might remain undisturbed. There, he spent days absorbed in such deep states of meditation that he was unaware of the constant bites of insects and pests. Seshadri Swamigal, a local saint, discovered him in the underground vault and tried to protect him. After about six weeks in the Patala-lingam, he was carried out and cleaned up. For the next two months he stayed in the Subramanya Shrine, so unaware of his body and surroundings that food had to be placed in his mouth or he would have starved.

In February 1897, six months after his arrival at Tiruvannamalai, Ramana moved to Gurumurtam, a temple about a mile away. Shortly after his arrival a sadhu named Palaniswami went to see him. Palaniswami's first sight of Ramana filled him with peace and bliss, and from that time on he served Ramana as his permanent attendant. Besides physical protection, Palaniswami would also beg for alms, cook and prepare meals for himself and Ramana, and care for him as needed.

Gradually, despite Ramana's desire for privacy, he attracted attention from visitors who admired his silence and austerities, bringing offerings and singing praises. Eventually a bamboo fence was built to protect him. During this time, his family had heard of his location and came to convince him to come home. Maharshi, however, just sat motionless until his family gave up their efforts.

Soon after this, in February 1899, Ramana left the foothills to live on Arunachala itself. He stayed briefly in Satguru Cave and Guhu Namasivaya Cave before taking up residence at Virupaksha Cave for the next 17 years.

In 1902, a government official named Sivaprakasam Pillai, with writing slate in hand, visited the young Swami in the hope of obtaining answers to questions about "How to know one's true identity." The fourteen questions put to the young Swami and his answers were Ramana's first teachings on Self-enquiry, the method for which he became widely known, and were eventually published as *Nan Yar?*, or in English, *Who am I?*

From 1922 until his death in 1950, Ramana lived in Sri Ramanasramam, the ashram that developed around his mother's tomb. In 1928, the so-called Old Hall was built, and it was here that Ramana lived until 1949. During this time, he spent most of his days in meditation, or giving teachings to whoever desired them. He never refused to share his wisdom with those who sought it, regardless of what time they visited him. Ramana slept in this hall, which was open twenty-four hours a day, so he could be of service to all who sought his help.

Ramana Maharshi was, and is, considered by many as an exceptional awakened being. His wisdom was profound, and his compassion was immense. When asked the question, "Who am I?" Maharshi replied by saying:

"The gross body which is composed of the seven humours (dhatus), I am not; the five cognitive sense organs—the senses of hearing, touch, sight, taste, and smell, which apprehend their respective objects—sound, touch, color, taste, and odor, I am not; the five cognitive sense-organs— the organs of speech, locomotion, grasping, excretion, and procreation, which have as their respective functions speaking, moving, grasping, excreting, and enjoying, I am not; the five vital airs, prana, etc., which perform respectively the five functions of in-breathing, etc., I am not; even the mind which thinks, I am not; the nescience too, which is endowed only with the residual impressions of

objects, and in which there are no objects and no functioning's, I am not.

Questioner: If I am none of these, then who am I?

Maharshi: After negating all of the above-mentioned as 'not this', 'not this', that Awareness which alone remains——that I am."

Ramana Maharshi, along with other mystics, realized that you cannot speak of the Self in positive terms, as no words can accurately describe what it is. Therefore, he spoke frequently in terms of negation—saying what awareness is not, in hopes that by removing all that is not oneself, one can reveal the pure awareness that they are. This process of negating reality to return to one's original being is called "*neti, neti*" in Sanskrit or "not this, nor that" in English.

It is an interesting experiment to try with oneself—to observe all of the things that we identify with, and to ask ourselves honestly if that is who we really are, or who we have believed ourselves to be. Many people identify themselves with their social roles—such as a mother, a father, a politician, a doctor, or whatever their career might be—but these roles are not who we are. The roles change constantly, and there are many roles we play throughout our lives, but we are not dependent on these roles.

Similarly, people identify with their gender, their race, their nationality, their religious beliefs, their social class, etc. none of these things can really define us, and by identifying with these different labels we only divide ourselves from one another. Nothing that exists outside of you can be your true Self, for your one and only identity is awareness, and that is something that we all share.

> *"Self is only Being – not this or that. It is Simple Being. BE, and that is the end of ignorance. Your duty is not to be this or that. I am that I am sums up the whole truth. The method is summed up in the words Be still. Be as you really are. Be yourself and nothing more. Remain aware of yourself and all else will be known"*
>
> —*Ramana Maharshi*

Ramana Maharshi did an amazing job at explaining with clarity and simplicity the truth of our Self as Awareness. According to Ramana, *"Everything is the Self. There is nothing but that… we are everywhere, we are all that is, and there is nothing else."*

In this statement Ramana is referring to the truth that at the core of every being, and in fact of existence itself, lies the One Self—pure consciousness. Like the many petals growing from the center of a flower, the numerous waves emerging from the great ocean, or the various rays shining from the central sun, we are but a myriad of beings arising from the pure beingness of the universe—one consciousness experiencing itself as many.

This understanding of the oneness of all beings in the universe was reflected in Ramana's words and actions. He knew that at the core of every being resided the Self, and that this was the same Self within his own heart. Understanding that every being is our Self experiencing unique situations and circumstances, naturally gives rise to understanding, love, and compassion for all living things. Thus, when posed with the question, *"how are we to treat others?"* Ramana replied simply, *"there are no others."*

11 LOVE

"The consciousness in you and the consciousness in me,
apparently two, really one, seek unity and that is love."
— *Sri Nisargadatta Maharaj*

If, at the center of every being lies this eternal Self of Consciousness, what exactly does this mean for us? What does it mean that the same energy that makes up my being, makes up your being, that the source of my awareness is the source of your awareness, and that we are all connected?

It means that the ideas we have of being separate from one another, the beliefs we use as a justification for harming the planet, or for acting selfishly, are nothing more than illusions produced by our ignorant perception of life. It means that in reality, we are all connected to life, and that harming any life harms all life, including "your" life. It means that when anyone acts violently towards another, they are really acting violently towards themselves. It means that no matter how we choose to perceive the world, the truth remains that we are bound to one another, and to all of creation, for all of existence is a manifestation of the same primordial spirit of consciousness.[1]

We have no choice but to love one another, look after one another, and take care of one another. When you see someone suffering, it is really you suffering in the form of that person. And when you compassionately send your love and care to that person, you are contributing that loving energy to all that exists.*

Love is the profound connection we feel when we realize our oneness with others, when you look into the eyes of another person and realize that person is you. Every being comes from the same life essence as you; they are the same consciousness, just inhabiting a different

---

* Some of the content of this chapter has been excerpted from my book "Oneness: Awakening From the Illusion of Separation."

form. Whether you are looking into the eyes of another human, a dog, a fish, or an insect, or whether you are feeling the presence of life in a plant, in the soil, or in a mineral, it makes no difference. It is all the same consciousness inhabiting a different form. Everything is you. All is Self.

Every being experiences themselves as the center of their experience. Consciousness is what lies at our very core, and connects us all to each other. We may appear to be separate and individual because of the various forms our Consciousness inhabits, but below the surface the substance of our being is one and the same.

Look into the eyes of another living being, any being—human, animal, insect—and you will see the same awareness looking back at you. The eyes have often been referred to as the gateway to the soul, and if you look into someone's eyes sincerely, without judging them, without being afraid of feeling vulnerable, you will see that indeed the eyes are the gateway to the soul. Looking into the eyes of another being, we see our Self staring back at us. As if we were looking into a mirror we see our own reflection.

If you practice looking beyond the surface of appearances—of body, behavior, personality, etc.—you will begin to see the true Being that lies within each form. You will see your Consciousness looking through the eyes of another, and it is when you see yourself in another that you cannot help but have compassion for them; because in Truth, there is no "them," there is no "other," there is only you, experiencing yourself from an inconceivable amount of perspectives.

We are only able to belittle, abuse, and harm one another, when we forget that the other person is us; when we only see the objects of form, and not the formless Consciousness that lies within each form. Lust, greed, violence, selfishness—all arise from perceiving others in terms of their individual differences, seeing them only as bodies, and what we can get from them as bodies, rather than acknowledging the Being that lies within the body.

When we see one another as different aspects of our Self—as our Self experiencing a different situation and circumstance—we develop a love, a connection, and a unity that allows us to see beyond the various forms, as well as the various ways that someone may act out when they have forgotten their formless nature. If you look at another in this light, you will see a Being that is just like you, looking back at you. It is the recognition of this oneness and connection with another that gives rise to what we call Love.

True Love is when you are able to see yourself in another, when you recognize that there is no separation between you and any other Being in the universe. Only forms can differ, and even then, all forms are dependent upon one another. In Truth, you are limitless, infinite, formless, and eternally connected to the Universe as a whole. Separation is an illusion.

You don't exist in the Universe; you are so intertwined with the Universe that you can be nothing but the Universe itself. Your true nature is consciousness, and this consciousness is connected to the consciousness of the Universe. Doing harm to any one of consciousness's manifestations—whether it be another person, animal, or plant—is essentially only causing harm to yourself.

All humans, animals, and plants are made up of cells that are alive and conscious. Their consciousness is arguably far more simple than our own, but it must exist at some level because they perform tasks and respond to their environment. They know that they must be doing whatever it is they are driven to do, but they do not see that billions of them come together to create a human, a plant, or an animal. In the same way, we are so focused on living our own individual lives that we are unaware we make up an entire organism called "Earth," and that we are its many cells, living together as one. Although currently, we behave as if we are a virus to the earth, slowly destroying the living organism that we are a part of, rather than ensuring its health and survival. This is of course a result of our ignorance and our failure to see how we and the Earth are one.

Galaxies, solar systems, planets, humans, animals, plants, minerals, cells, molecules, atoms—we are layer upon layer of the universe experiencing itself as what appears to be separate entities that are really all one and the same. To use an analogy: The Universe is a tree, and we are all its leaves. Each leaf is kept alive by the total energy of the tree, but from its own perspective, the leaf seems as if it were separate from the rest of the leaves, and even the tree itself. And what spiritual teachers refer to as "Enlightenment" is simply the realization that the leaf is connected to the tree as a whole, as are all of the leaves, and that the true nature of the leaf is the entire tree.

The leaf cannot be without the tree. In reality, there is no separation. Love is the feeling that we have when we can see that we are not separate from the other leaves, that we are all creations of the tree from which we emerged. When you can see another as a reflection of yourself, then you have compassion for them, and this kind of compassion for others is what is truly needed to heal the world.

We never really know the circumstances that others are experiencing. But knowing that we have suffered, enables us to see that others suffer just like we do. People often hide their suffering and look as if they are not suffering on the surface, but deep down they may be in great pain. Knowing that everyone experiences suffering in their own way, and that all beings have a common desire to be happy, should inspire us to do our best to free people from their suffering, to be kind to others at all times, because even the smallest act of kindness can feel like a breath of fresh air to someone who is suffocating from their suffering.

We cannot continue to exist with so much violence, so much disrespect, so much fear and judgment toward others; we are only hurting ourselves by doing this. Our actions ripple out into the Universe, creating a chain of events that affects every single particle in existence. Actions driven by love benefit more than just us or those in direct contact with our actions, they benefit the whole of existence.

Any actions that are driven by fear, violence, anger, hatred, jealousy, or greed, are produced by a mind that is dominated by ego and selfish motives. If we realized our connection to one another and to the source of all life, we would act only in love, always having the health of life as a whole in mind. In order to feel the love that comes from understanding our oneness, we have to let go of the idea that we are separate. We have to see clearly that we are not the ego personality, the ego is just a thought that the brain, and by extension the Universe, is having. To say it from a Christian's perspective: We must surrender ourselves (our ideas of being a separate self) in order to receive the love of God.

The notion that we are separate from the rest of existence causes us to cling to life out of fear. We cling to the world because we fail to realize that we are the world, and it is this ignorant perception of life that has produced our misconception of what love really is. Many people confuse love with attachment, which is a quality of fear— the fear of loss—and it results in insecurity and dependency, which has been the cause of many broken hearts and failed relationships.

The qualities of fear are attachment, dependency, and resistance. The qualities of love are appreciation, understanding, and acceptance. We can observe very easily in our personal relationships whether we are acting out of fear or love. Looking at an intimate relationship with a partner for example, if we are selfish, clingy, jealous, spiteful, mistrusting, dependent, etc., our relationship is composed primarily of fear or ego. If, however we are selfless, understanding, accepting, appreciative, caring, supportive and trusting, our relationship is composed primarily of love or spirit. All emotions are essentially produced by feelings of either fear or love; either seeing ourselves as the ego—separate; or understanding our existence as consciousness—one.

Fear and our idea of separation produce feelings of attachment, resistance, anxiety, anger, violence, hatred, jealousy, envy, and depression. Love and our understanding of oneness produce feelings of freedom,

JOSEPH P. KAUFFMAN

acceptance, security, calmness, peace, understanding, gratitude, trust, compassion, and happiness.

Observe within yourself whether your relationships are driven by fear or love. Do you really love the other person in the relationship? Meaning, do you really want what is best for them, regardless of whether that involves you in their life? Or do you just wish to control this person for your own benefit? If your love is only a will to possess, it is not love.

Observe how you interact with other human beings, animals, and plants. Do you care for these living beings or do you just wish to use them for your benefit, and otherwise have no interest or care at all? Do you judge others based on their appearance or the form they inhabit? They cannot help the way they look, and the way they look has nothing to do with who they really are. What sense does it make to judge someone because they look, think, or behave differently than you? What benefit do you get from that? None. Only the ego—the illusory identity formed by the belief in separation—benefits from judgment by enforcing its idea of separation and strengthening its self-image. But you are not the ego, and the views of separation that stem from a mind dominated by ego are not composed of love.

Love is not controlling. Love is not restricting, limiting, or exclusive. Love is free. Love is relaxing, sincere, and inclusive. Love is the energy that we need to embody in order to heal the planet, society, and ourselves. We need to align our state of being with love in order to find peace. We must let go of the conditioning and ignorant beliefs that have caused us to act from a view of fear and separation, and begin acting from an understanding of love, connection, and oneness. Love is the only thing that is truly capable of healing the state of the world.

If we are to live in love, and act according to the understanding of our oneness, then we need to make the reality of our oneness something we feel deep in our hearts. This understanding needs to be the at the very core of our being, the foundation for all our thoughts, and the motivating force behind all of our actions. For this to happen, we need to individually contemplate, think, and meditate upon this truth until it becomes clear to us. We need to inquire into the nature of Self, understand the oneness of Self, and abide as the Self. If we can understand and live this truth in our daily lives, all of our actions will stem from this understanding of our oneness, and naturally we will begin living in a way that benefits the whole of existence.

12   ABIDING AS THE SELF

"Once you realize that your true nature is pure Awareness, the next 'step' is abiding as this pure undefinable, ungraspable, unknowable-yet-somehow-still-knowable awareness that you are.
Seeking is doing. Abiding is being."

—*Michael Jeffreys*

To abide as the Self, we need to first realize the Self, and shed away all of the things that prevent us from being as we truly are. The good news is that you are already your Self, and there is nothing you really need to 'do' to become what you already are. We are used to 'doing'—our whole society is constantly 'doing,' constantly moving, constantly running about frantically and full of stress. We are always looking for something to do, something to accomplish. We even feel shameful or guilty when we aren't being productive, so even when we have time to relax we are thinking about what to do next.

There is nothing you need to 'do' to realize the Self. You 'do' enough. No, instead you simply have to 'be.' Allow yourself to just be as you are, in your natural state, and let everything else pass away—then see what remains. When everything else has gone—what is left? Find out for yourself.

The Self is pure Being, it is your Being, your Self. To know it you just have to be. Be the awareness that you are, the witness, the observer, the consciousness. Understand that you cannot observe your Self—for you are the Self that is observing. See if you can rest in this state of pure observing, pure witnessing, pure presence, pure consciousness.

We find difficulty in simply being the pure and impartial witness, because our conditioning has caused us to be so entangled in our minds that we are distracted by every thought, consumed by every emotion, pulled by every desire. Our society is full of distractions. Everything is constantly luring our attention outwards—phones, computers, televisions, video games, advertisements, magazines, social obligations etc.—so much so that the simple suggestion to look within is seen as a mystical and impractical task.

Why is it that so many people find difficulty in looking within themselves and observing their own minds? We act as if we would rather be victims of our restless and untamed minds, than observe our minds and be free.

People have identified themselves with the contents of their minds—with their ego, their beliefs about the world, their ideas of who they are, their fantasies about the future, regrets about the past, the things they like and dislike, their countless desires and expectations, etc. We are so involved in our minds and frequent mental stimulation, that we are afraid of what might happen when the mind is quiet.

If we sit in silence, our mental content begins to fade away, and everything we have clung to for identity and security begins to reveal its illusory nature. This frightens us, and so rarely ever do we sit in silence. We have become so engulfed in the noise of the world that we are afraid of the silence within us.

But the truth can only be realized in silence. In silence, our true nature reveals itself—and it is far more profound than words can convey or thought can imagine. It can only be known through experience— your own experience—and once you experience this great and mysterious truth, from the depths of your being will come forth a silent-knowing, a deep trust in the universe, an understanding that all is well, and a peace that follows you everywhere you go. In the Bible, this peace is referred to as the *"peace which passeth all understanding,"* because it is a peace that has no logical explanation, but is nonetheless experientially present and profound.

Once you realize this peace you will understand the meaning of Lao Tzu's statement that, *"Those who speak do not know. Those who know do not speak."* For the infinite truth is, and will always be, beyond the scope of finite words and explanations.

The way of realizing this truth that is emphasized by all of the great mystics, is through the practices of meditation and self-inquiry. Meditation is the art of quieting the mind, or emptying the mind of its content, in order for awareness to abide in/as itself. However, do not think you have to force out all thoughts to realize your witnessing Self. Instead, imagine that your awareness is like space, and that the thoughts and sensations which arise are like objects floating in this spaciousness. Just as space contains all things within it, but is unaffected by everything it contains, so too does awareness contain every thought, sensation, and experience, yet remains untouched by these phenomena at all times. Allowing your mind to be like space, things will come and go as they please—arising and dissolving in spaciousness—and you will be unaffected by them as long as you do not invest any interest and emotion into what arises. Then, over time, the thoughts will subside and become quieter, and consciousness will be able to rest as it is—spacious, open, and ever-present.

Meditation is not done to achieve a goal. It is not done to become Self-realized, as contradictory as this may sound. Meditation is simply allowing the Self to be the Self, and through that we come to understand the reality of who we are—and the unreality of who we have believed ourselves to be.

As the great Zen master Dogen said, *"Meditation is not a way to enlightenment, Nor is it a method of achieving anything at all. It is peace itself. It is the actualization of wisdom, The ultimate truth of the oneness of all things."* To meditate for the sake of achieving a goal goes against the very art of meditation. Meditation is being as you are, being aware, letting go of achievement, of wishing, of hoping, of doing, wanting, planning, analyzing, straining, striving, fantasizing, imagining, thinking, etc.

This does not mean you can never achieve anything, hope for anything, do anything, plan for anything, or think about anything if you practice meditation. But we are constantly involved in some form of mental activity. Haven't you ever wondered what remains when all of the activity of the mind has ceased?

If you are identified with your mind, then the cessation of thought is equivalent to death, and so subconsciously, meditation will be a source of great fear to you. However, if you are willing to see beyond the mind, and discover the very source of the mind—

the eternal awareness that you are—then meditation is your greatest companion.

Meditation shows us the reality of who we are, and teaches us that we can find immense bliss in simply being as we are without constantly trying to escape ourselves. Have you ever heard the saying, "wherever you go, there you are"? Well, it's true—no matter what you do or where you go, *you* are still there. Who is the *you* that is there? Who is the *you* beneath all of the noise of the mind?

Meditation is not a practice in which we do anything. It is a practice in which we stop doing, in which we stop completely, both inwardly and outwardly, in order to reconnect with our source and realize the fundamental ground of our Being.

Meditation is the art of resting and relaxing. When we relax completely our thoughts start to dissipate, and we become aware of their transitory nature. When we try to meditate to reach some goal, we only add onto the concepts and illusions that we are trying to see through. If we meditate as an attempt to get rid of our ego, it is only because the ego thinks it will be better because of it. The ego—the fearful and conditioned part of ourselves that clings to the mind for a sense of identity—so easily disguises itself by shifting its identification with a spiritual path. This is one of the ego traps that so many people easily fall into.

Many spiritual traditions attempt to eliminate the ego, and think that they have to resist the ego and fight it, but this only strengthens the ego. The more we try to transcend it, the stronger it becomes, because we are asserting its reality instead of recognizing its illusory nature. As Chuang Tzu said, *"Is not your elimination of self a positive manifestation of self?... Why then these vain struggles... as though beating a drum in search of a fugitive?"*

Therefore, we should just let go of our effort to conquer and get rid of the illusion and just relax. When we connect to a state of presence—of being fully attentive to the moment—the ego naturally dissolves in our loving awareness, without us having to do anything. It really is that simple.

In fact, it is because the truth is so simple that so many people have difficulty in realizing it. The mind desires for an answer that is more complex, more technical, more conceptual—but this is only so it can know and understand it intellectually, which provides the mind with the illusion of control and security. All we need to do is stop this mental clinging to concepts and forms, and deeply relax into the present moment.

When we do this, the stuff of the mind begins to dissolve into our awareness, like grains of salt dissolving into the great ocean. Don't be afraid of silence, it is the secret to discovering your true Self.

We can read about meditation all that we want. We can think about it. We can plan our next meditation. We can visualize it. We can form opinions and beliefs about it. But none of these efforts will help us actually experience meditation. We have to take that step and look within ourselves. We have to face our inner reality, and observe what is preventing us from being at peace in this moment. If we want to discover our true nature, we have to explore the reality that is present when the mind is silent and undistracted.

People are afraid of silence, afraid of the unknown, and find safety in what is known and familiar. Thus, many people would rather cling to their illusions—even if they cause them suffering—than embrace the unknown reality of each moment. Life is unknown for life is always changing. We can cling to our thoughts of stability and security if we want, but it will only cause pain later on when the reality of life's changing nature interferes with our desire for permanence.

Instead of fearing the unknown and resisting change, we can be receptive to the change of life, attentive to each new moment, flexible and adaptive to what comes and goes, and we can find the changeless Self within us and abide in the peace that it provides.

The notion that the psychological self we hold so dearly is really an illusion of the mind, is something that is often very difficult to come to terms with, as we have invested so much time and energy into this illusory self. But if one gets even a glimpse of this truth, they can no longer be fooled by their mental illusions—try as they may.

All of our habits are rooted in this belief, and carry with them a tremendous amount of momentum, compelling us to carry out the same old patterns, even after we have discovered new truths. We feel safe and comfortable in our habits, and part of us wants to remain stagnant in these habits. But our heart knows there is more, and once you have glimpsed your true nature, it becomes harder and harder to follow the same habitual patterns, as you now see through their illusory nature.

While these habits carry a strong energy that influences us to keep repeating them, we also choose to stay in these habits out of fear, which results in clinging and attachment. We are afraid of losing our self, because we have confused the illusory self with our true Self, but in clinging to our illusory self we are really just masking ourselves from the reality of our true being. But when we surrender our self-centered experience, what we get in return is the whole universe. When we let go of our constant mental activity and self-talk, we open ourselves up fearlessly to the eternal continuum of the here and now.

Surrender is of great importance here. To surrender is to no longer hold on, to no longer resist and fight. When we surrender, we accept the moment deeply, giving up our resistance, and releasing our attempt to battle against reality. Surrender the mind and its need to have everything figured out—the mind is limited to its past experience, knowledge and memory. It is limited by perception, and cannot know that which is beyond perception, that which perceives. It can never grasp our true nature like it grasps a concept or belief. We have to surrender this way of understanding, and realize that there is another way of knowing the truth, a way that is centered in the intuition of our heart. A way that is known through our very being. As the great sage Lao Tzu said in the Tao Te Ching, *"you cannot know it, but you can be it, at ease in your own life."*

According to Christian doctrine, we must surrender ourselves to God—we must surrender our ego self and its desire for security and control, to the eternal awareness and presence that we are. To truly surrender your ego to the greater intelligence that operates through you and through all beings is an act of faith, which brings with it a sense of trust in the course of nature, and a relationship with the intelligence of the universe. It is a beautiful experience that allows us to let go of the weight we carry and trust in our original nature.

The description of this with language is nowhere near the reality of experiencing it for oneself, but hopefully it can offer some insight. You do not ever need to be afraid of losing yourself. Because whatever can leave you is not the true you. If you feel you are losing yourself, it is because you are identified with what is not your essential Self. If the you that you think you are disappears, where does it go, and who/what remains? It is a fascinating thing to explore, and what awaits you in this exploration is a love, a peace, and a freedom that transcends all description.

Explore the silence. Practice being the witness. Become aware of your thoughts, your habitual reactions, your tendency to cling to thoughts and emotions. Allow the noise of the mind to be there, and to come and go as it pleases, but remain centered in your awareness. If you have no interest in the thoughts and emotions, and do not feed them with more thoughts, but just remain as the passive witness, then gradually the thoughts will fade away, and you will stand free as you are—the eternal and pure consciousness at the source of all being.

As you meditate in this way, observing the mental content as it fades away, it is helpful to have a sense of what you are falling into—or rather what is being revealed. There has to be an element of trust in your true Self, or else your subconscious fears may prevent you from going deeper.

We have been running away from ourselves for so long, and there are so many thoughts, emotions, memories, and traumas that we have yet to acknowledge, yet to accept, and yet to forgive. These will likely come up when you stop escaping yourself and simply sit to observe. Know that these will pass too. Feel the emotions that arise, sit with them, feel them, observe them, forgive them, let them go, but don't cling to them or let them overcome you. Be the observer and allow the thoughts and emotions to liberate themselves, and to fade away in their own time.

Be aware of everything that arises until you realize that you are awareness itself. Familiarize yourself with this awareness and abide in it. Through the practice of meditation, we can free our minds from our conditioning—simply because we are no longer consumed by it or ignorant of it, but have created the space between us and our minds, allowing us to observe our minds and our conditioned thought patterns, allowing them to be released, and allowing ourselves to be free.

Don't think that meditation is limited to just sitting—that meditation is just sitting for thirty minutes, and then you get up and stop meditating. Carry meditation into every aspect of your life. Live your life in a meditative manner. Reclaim your mind from habitual patterns. Don't just live your life on auto-pilot, but become aware of life, become aware of your relationship with life.

Meditation can easily be brought into everyday tasks. When you eat, eat with awareness. When you walk, walk with awareness. When you talk, talk with awareness. Perhaps the best way to maintain awareness in daily life is to simply be aware of your breath. Notice your breath while you are eating, while you are moving, while you are driving, or working, or whatever it is you may be doing. The breath helps anchor us into the present moment, so that we can be aware of what is here and now, rather than being lost in our unnecessary thinking.

As you go about your day, notice your habitual reactions. Observe what triggers an emotional response in you. Why is that there? Where does it come from? Notice these reactions, and see if instead of reacting to life, you can learn how to respond to life with awareness.

The more you practice bringing awareness into daily life, the more you will realize just how unaware you have been. The majority of human beings live as if they are sleepwalking, running on autopilot, unaware of their thoughts and actions, behaving primarily out of habit and conditioning. The very essence of a spiritual or meditative practice is to be free of ignorance and conditioning by bringing awareness to all areas of life, and realizing your true Self as awareness, as presence, as being. This is what it means to awaken—to become aware, to wake up from the sleep-like state we have lived in for so long, and to be sensitive and in touch with the reality of life.

As Sri Amma Bhagavan said, *"All spiritual growth lies on the bedrock of awareness."* We are that bedrock of awareness, and by bringing awareness into our lives we are really reconnecting with our true essence. Once you have learned to abide in your true Self, you can live freely in this world without being a victim of it. You remain centered in your Self, and unaffected by the pleasures and pains that arise from the changing nature of reality. As many mystics have described it, you are free to live *in* the world, but are not *of* the world—you are present to the world, but are not dependent upon it for your peace, as you have found the source of peace within your very own being.

By understanding the source of your being, you understand the source of all being. Through this deep understanding, compassion flourishes, as you see your essential Self as the Self in all.

The essential, irreducible nature of experience is the consciousness that shines in each one of us as the experience of being aware. This awareness is the aspect of experience that cannot be removed, and is shared by all beings. It is equally available to all people, at all times and under all circumstances, regardless of age, gender, race, nationality, or religion.

It is the foundation of inner peace, and thus it must be the foundation of world peace as well. If we, as individuals, can awaken to this peace within, then naturally it will create peace in the world.

All that is required is for us to realize that our own fundamental existence is shared with the existence of all beings and things, and to live the implications of this realization in all realms of life. Once we shift our definition of Self to include all beings, then the world can heal, then we can live in harmony, then we can live in peace.

> *"Love the world as yourself; then you can care for all things."*
>
> —*Lao Tzu*

About the Author

Joseph P. Kauffman is the founder of Conscious Collective, LLC—an organization dedicated to the awakening of human consciousness. A yoga and meditation teacher, breathwork facilitator, and herbal medicine practitioner, Joseph is devoted to helping others heal from their conditioning, and realize their true nature and essential oneness with the whole of nature.

www.conscious-collective.com

Made in the USA
Lexington, KY
10 December 2018